Geoff Hart is a freelance novelist and poet with a particular interest in Bulgaria. He has written two novels, a historical novel, *The Icon of Arbanasi,* set in the seventeenth century and *Second Time Lucky* set twenty years into the future. *Bulgaria: Unfinished Business* is his only work of non-fiction to date.

CW01511904

BULGARIA: UNFINISHED BUSINESS

GEOFF HART

Bulgaria – Unfinished Business
Geoff Hart

This book is based on my recollection of events and conversations from my memories of them.

The moral right of the author has been asserted

ACKNOWLEDGMENTS

I did not have to research this book as I have been living it since 2004, but certain people helped me see things clearly during that time. So for their help and friendship I would like to thank Georgi Koev, Rositsa Ilieva, Dimitrina Pavlova, Nicolay Nicolaev, and Desislava Ivanovo.

We spent a long time preparing for our journey with the horses in 2014 and many people offered helpful advice for which I am grateful. My friends in the Fox Inn, Ysceifiog gave a lot of earnest advice about taking animals abroad. Some spoke from experience and others from the inherent wisdom of the pub goer. All was well intentioned and for that I am grateful. However, for consistent good sense and practical advice from someone who knew I would particularly like to thank Helen Burrows.

Thanks go to Mandi Hill for the first and therefore the hardest proof read and for going beyond her brief to make useful comments on phrasing and style. Many thanks go to Mark Lee and Lucy Hart for their critical reader comments and additional thanks to Lucy for her general advice throughout.

A number of friends and family members read the book and told me that it was good. Whether this opinion was genuine or based on friendship and family loyalty does not matter because it encouraged me anyway. While I was writing this book someone had to take more than their fair share of the horse chores and for that I am grateful to my wife, Marieluise, but I particularly want to thank her for never doubting.

For Tony, my fellow adventurer (1949-2009)

And for Dima who has made my life in Bulgaria possible

viii

Table of Contents

x

2014: The Journey Begins

Saturday 29th March 2014: Departure

The year would end with us living with our horses in the foothills of the Balkan Mountains, but today after all the planning the adventure of a lifetime starts here at our North Wales home, Silver Rake.

Packing up the horsebox yesterday I had an onslaught of emotions: trepidation, excitement, but most of all funny feelings about leaving our home. We may not have realised it, but Silver Rake is in our blood; it is part of us and we are part of its four hundred year history. The name comes from the open caste silver and lead mine that was previously on the site along with the house. It is the only house in the area with an English name and that is because it was originally owned by London Quakers. I haven't even talked to my wife, Marieluise about the thoughts I have been preoccupied with, but my guess is she is experiencing the same feelings. We have spent nearly thirty years making this place what it is and it must remain ours wherever we travel and whatever we do. As horse owners we have everything we need at Silver Rake: six acres of good quality grassland with a large field shelter, three stone built stables in front of the house on a large yard and a sand ménage for training the horses. And we have a beautiful house with our lovely daughters and their families nearby.

Despite our immense attachment to our current home we are moving with our dog and two of our three horses, Flo and Guinness, to a farmhouse in the mountains of central Bulgaria which we have also fallen in love with. "Why are you doing it?", so many of our friends have asked. On one level it's an easy question to answer: the weather is beautiful and everything is so cheap. We are outdoor people living in a part of the UK where being outside is often a massive struggle against the elements. Also keeping and competing with horses in the UK has become a very expensive hobby. That is the simple answer and this indeed forms a big part of our reasoning, but there is so much more to it than that.

Bulgaria is in many ways a new country. For virtually the first time in the country's turbulent history, Bulgarians are in charge of their own destiny as a newly democratic state. On the other hand it is a country with proud traditions that its people are anxious to maintain. In short it is an exciting place to be where progress and positive change can be seen almost daily. Also it offers a massive life style change. It is a beautiful and sparsely populated country with vast swathes of forest and wide sweeping mountain ranges. The pace of life is slow and people have time. The seasons are well defined and you can enjoy outdoor life from early spring to late autumn. As an emerging state Bulgaria has its problems, but it has a great deal to offer. I have been involved with the country for more than ten years and I love it.

Having cleared up in my mind, that today is the start of an adventure, not a permanent farewell to the past, I started to feel more relaxed. Because of that I felt I was going about everything in a dead organised matter of fact way. And I think Marieluise felt the same. So how come we got up at five thirty and left at nine twenty? Obviously we weren't as on top of our emotions as we thought. So we left at nine twenty, stopped ten miles from home on the A55 for fuel and along with dog and horses were properly on our way before ten, not as we had hoped but OK.

The trip we are making is quite daunting. Starting from North Wales we travel to Dover to catch the ferry to Calais. From France we travel through Belgium and Holland and into Germany. We then travel in a south easterly direction right through Germany into Austria and on to Hungary. From here the shortest route is through Serbia. However, the documentation required to travel in a lorry with horses and dogs is mind boggling. We did not want to make it even more complicated by straying outside the European Union. Therefore from Hungary we intend to enter Romania and travel south east into Bulgaria via a bridge across the Danube. We have altogether eight scheduled overnight stops on a journey of three thousand, six hundred kilometres.

After two short breaks, one on the M6 Toll road and one on the M1 near Luton, we arrived at the stables we had booked near Waltham Abbey at about five thirty for our first overnight stop. We drove down a narrow road through the forest and turned into a yard teaming with life; kids with parents, adult riders, staff, and horses and ponies of all shapes and sizes including one the size of a Labrador! One look at the automobiles parked in the car park told us that riding is still a rich person's sport in the South East of England, no ten pound a week DIY livery here. My guess is that full livery is in the region of two hundred pound per week. London really is a country within a country as Marieluise has become fond of saying.

After all the emotional energy we had spent at the beginning of the day we were both shattered. Sounds ridiculous, but we were in bed by seven forty five and probably asleep by eight. During the night my attempts at al-fresco weeing were undermined by a series of security lights that were activated by the slightest movement including the surreptitious lowering of a zip, so I resigned myself to the trek to the toilet elegantly clad in a fleece, underpants and black leather town shoes. Therefore when I needed the loo for the second time at about five thirty I decided to get up and make tea.

Sunday 30th March 2014: Waltham Abbey, near London to Beek, Holland

The clocks going forward meant that it was actually six thirty when I made tea and as it proved the clock remained against us for the remainder of the day.

One thing I didn't mention on day one was the layout of our horsebox. It is a seven and a half tonne truck with an enclosed cab. Behind the cab is a side entrance to the area where we are living, cooking and sleeping. Further back again is a large area where the horses travel. We can access this area through a sliding door from the living space and the horses enter via a ramp at the back of the vehicle. It is a very large piece of kit and when I first got behind the wheel I was surprised that I was allowed to drive it on an ordinary licence. Now driving it feels more comfortable. During travel all our stuff -

3

mainly horse stuff – completely fills the living area. So after stabling the horses and before we can eat or sleep ourselves we have to put everything into the horse area. Of course before doing this we have to thoroughly clean the horses' accommodation – Marieluise is fanatical and even cleans the walls as well as the floor. Before setting off in the morning we have to put all the stuff back into the living area to free up the back space for the horses. Sounds terrible; I suppose it is but there is no alternative way of doing things. So this morning we did all of this as well as the normal chores associated with horses and then were informed that, despite paying sixty five pounds for one night's livery, we were required to muck out. After everything else Flo, our young piebald mare, would not load and so we left at about ten thirty.

Within half an hour of leaving our planned route was disturbed by a collision that closed the road. We managed to avoid turning that way causing the satnav to have a nervous breakdown. After several attempts to make me do a U-turn, alright in a Fiat 500, but not so good in a 7.5 tonne wagon – the satnav plotted a new course. To cut a long story short we did not get on the ferry until twenty to four in the afternoon; add to that the fact that French time lost us another hour, we left Calais behind us at about seven with the light fading and about two hundred miles to go.

The traffic through Belgium was horrendous - so much for travelling on a Sunday! We got to the yard at Beek in the Netherlands at one thirty in the morning. Thank God it was a commercial horse transport yard so we just let ourselves in, found the stables that had been allocated to our horses and all was well, but what a day. This must be the worst it can get so we will put it behind us. Tomorrow will be a much easier day, I think. The good thing about today was the ferry crossing. We used to do this all the time forty years ago and it was always awful; Marieluise sick each time. Now you don't feel a single wave, progress on one front at least.

At two in the morning I should have gone to bed – Marieluise did, but I drank three cans of beer and then went for a wander 'round the yard. I was greeted by a Dutch chap at about three thirty with a hearty "Good Morning". He was loading horses to set off and I was not yet in bed. Well tomorrow is another day.

2004: Back to the Beginning

3rd April 2004

For some time my friend Tony and I had been looking, mainly on the net, at all the publicity regarding Bulgarian property. We had discussed it at great length and concluded that if you got in early enough there could be money to be made from purchasing some property at the current prices and selling them at a later date. The only flaw was that we knew almost nothing about the country and with the exception of reports about cheap houses there was very little information out there. There was only one way to resolve this and that was to take a look. Anyway, we anticipated that it might be fun.

We landed at Sofia International airport just after midday. We passed through customs and passport control where we had the relatively unusual experience of having our passport stamped. Above each booth there was a sign in Bulgarian and in English saying, "Do not pay any money to this official". Obviously it was the passengers' responsibility to ensure that no bribery took place, not the passport officers'! We moved on into the surprisingly small luggage collection hall and immediately got our first taste of Bulgarian efficiency. A bell rang and the sign above the first carousel (there were only two) illuminated and indicated that cases from the Manchester flight would be appearing soon. The old carousel lumbered into action and after the same solitary case had passed by three times the crowd started to get restless. One man on our flight however had obviously been here before and with a superior air he collected his case from carousel number two. Soon the rest of us caught on and Tony and I grabbed our cases and headed for the arrival lounge.

Now Sofia is the capital city of Bulgaria and this was the main international airport, but you could have been forgiven for thinking you had somehow stumbled into a small regional airport shortly before it was de-commissioned. To describe it as small and shabby would be to miss the essential spirit of the place. There were hoardings advertising cigarettes that surely had not existed for several decades,

Lucky Strike and Capstan full strength for example. There was just one food and drink outlet that seemed to sell nothing but coffee from an extremely thin collapsible plastic cup, bottles of water and coke in nineteen sixties glass bottles. I tell a lie, there were also bags of boiled sweets. At least there was no queue. A glance at the arrivals and departure boards told its own tale. There were in total no more than five flights arriving at or leaving the capital city in a twenty four hour period and one of those was an internal flight to Varna. So although all travel restrictions had been lifted on Bulgarian citizens since the end of Communism, they had not yet decided where they wanted to go and equally not many people were coming to have a look at them.

Once we got outside the whole nature of the place was transformed. Despite the fact that only a few flights were expected at the airport on this day there were at least a hundred taxis eager to greet and transport those brave or foolish enough to make the trip. What a noise they made! In the UK taxis at airports park in a queue and the first fare goes to the taxi at the front of the line. In Bulgaria there is no system of priority and every driver thrusts themselves forward yelling above the din with a plaintive appeal to you to get into their cab. The clever ones employ their own hustler who can mount the airport steps and grab the passengers before they reach the line of cabs and steer them towards their driver. We fell into this trap like flies into the spider's web and were whisked away by a young man driving an unmarked Opel Kadett that was almost certainly not a taxi.

We headed off towards the city centre, not quite knowing what to expect other than that it would be different from other UK and European cities that we knew. In some ways this was true and in other ways not so. Like in most cities there were a variety of buildings from different eras, some grand, some mundane; some beautiful and some hideously ugly. What was peculiar to Sofia though was the overwhelming impression of grey. The city was almost devoid of bright lights and most of the shops looked closed, although we were later to discover that this was not the case. Every single building looked tired and in need of work ranging from complete renovation to at the very least a lick of paint. This applied to shops and businesses, public buildings and residential properties alike. The most striking reminder that Bulgaria was until recently a Communist state was to be found at each roundabout and major crossroad in the city. Overlooking each junction was a high watchtower with three or four armed state security guards at the top just watching. But what or who were they watching? And, now that the Committee for State Security had been disbanded, who were they reporting to? I imagined them filling out reports and filing them, all to no purpose. They must still be receiving a salary so I guess until someone tells them otherwise or just stops paying them they will keep up the surveillance of their fellow citizens although nobody is interested any longer in what they are doing or what they see.

To a westerner it gave the whole city an eerie feel. Just what effect it continued to have on Sofia citizens I could not judge, but, knowing them as I now do, I would guess that it was just another ludicrous legacy that they didn't even try to explain. Whereas we westerners need and demand an explanation of almost everything we see and experience, Bulgarians share with other post-Communist citizens an air of resignation which we find hard to understand.

The fare was sixty leva which seemed quite expensive. In fact we were to discover that this was about six times the standard price! Anyway we were dropped as requested at the train station. It was now about two in the afternoon and our train, an overnight sleeper to Varna, was not due to leave, according to Tony's research, until quarter to eleven. However, we had decided to get there early, check things out, buy our ticket and hopefully drop our cases off. The station was a grey sombre building on the edge of the city. We went in and found ourselves immediately alongside the tracks. Every track ended there so we concluded that there were no trains passing through the city. All the tracks were surprisingly rusty with grass and weeds growing between them. The interior of the station building was worn out and dirty. The departure board showed just three trains: one to Varna in half an hour, the next one to Bourgas in about three hours' time and then our overnight train to Varna due, as Tony had said, at ten forty five. We were now learning fast the lesson that had begun at the airport: Bulgarians don't travel very much, or at least not by train or plane.

We looked around for a ticket office, but to no avail. We then tried to identify where we could leave our luggage which proved equally fruitless. All we found was an office with three Soviet style middle-aged women inside. Each one appeared to look roughly the same: a heavy frame with an almost square head and short-cropped hair dyed red like a bad hair day nightmare. We tried the door; it was locked. We tapped gently on the glass emitting as we did two winning smiles, we felt sure would be hard to resist. How wrong we were. One member of the group did not even look up. The other two looked towards the source of the knocking and finding nothing there of interest or concern returned to their work. I do not know what railway business they were conducting, but it was clearly no business of ours. "Probably a customer relations seminar." Tony quipped. If it was they obviously had no intention of carrying out any fieldwork.

We were feeling somewhat stumped and were just wondering how to penetrate the secret world of Sofia station without getting arrested when a confident voice in clear, though accented English enquired, "Can I help you, English gentlemen?" The answer given by Tony was one with which I was to become familiar. "Welsh!" he exclaimed. "Of course," said Bulgaria's version of Charles Dickens' Uriah Heep. "What can I do for you nice Welsh gentlemen?" I decided not to prolong the scene by saying "English!" and instead explained what we wanted. It was already clear to me that this would cost us money, but as we seemed to be unable to make progress without help I couldn't see what else to do.

We followed our self-appointed guide downstairs into the bowels of the station building. We came out into a large poorly lit hall and our obsequious little helper pointed out a ticket office in the corner. Tony decided the time had come to take back the reins. He purposefully strode towards what purported to be a ticket office and in a clear Welsh voice made his request. "Two single first class tickets to Varna on the overnight sleeper, if you would be so kind?" To say that he was met with blank faces would be to overstate the level of engagement that came in response to his question. It would be more accurate to say that his presence was not in any way shape or form acknowledged. His temper was rising and so my suggestion to try it again in Welsh was not immediately appreciated.

Just as I feared a hole would appear in the glass booth before us, Uriah Heep stepped forward to save the day. At once the tickets were forthcoming along with the reservations for a sleeping berth. Tony tried to confirm that this was a two berth compartment. From the fact that the little chap just wrung his hands and said, "Please." we assumed it wasn't. Before he handed the tickets over the little man scrutinised them. I think he was checking whether the price was printed on the tickets, not wanting the opportunity to overcharge us to pass by unnecessarily. The price was indeed on the ticket and we found that an overnight sleeper in a first class carriage on a train travelling nearly six hundred kilometres could be purchased in Bulgaria for approximately four pounds! Step one was complete and our personal railway expert now lead us confidently further down into the depths of the building, presumably heading for the left luggage office or a set of lockers.

The room we arrived at was even more remote than the ticket office and was similarly unlit within. We could dimly make out a randomly stacked pile of suitcases at the back of the room. This time Tony did not interfere and when told to do so we graciously handed over our bags in return for two small pieces of recycled toilet paper on which the antiquated printer had made little impression. We assumed these would be required to redeem our bags and our guide confirmed this. I carefully placed the fragile tickets in a compartment of my wallet and with a satisfied smile I confirmed with Tony that our business was for the time being complete. It was now quarter to three in the afternoon and I am sure that without our little friend's able assistance we would still have been wandering around Sofia station at midnight. However, this did not mean that we were ready to be ripped off. "How much do we owe you?" I enquired in a business-like manner. "I really want to help you nice people, but maybe twenty leva would allow you to help me in return." In comparison the single first class ticket to Varna had cost twelve leva. This was too much. I was about to open polite negotiations when Tony took a ten leva note from his pocket and thrust it at the little chap. "That's all you are getting-now piss off!" Our guide started to object, but thought better of it and crawled away. For our part we headed upwards towards the light to seek out a Bulgarian bar.

We ended up in a beautiful open air bar that covered a good proportion of a large park near the city centre. Our errands done for the day all we had to do was relax and wait for the departure of our train. We had a salad and a bowl of chips and a couple of beers. The sky was a deep blue and the sun was warm although it was only early April. The young woman waiting at our table looked like a goddess. Everything was set fair for a very pleasant late afternoon and evening. As we sat there with inane grins settling across our features the waitress approached and in a manner more business-like than goddess-like told us we must settle our bill. We looked around us. Nobody seemed to be moving and at some tables waiters and waitresses were taking fresh orders. We were bemused. "We had been planning to stay for a while yet." I ventured. "You pay now, please" was the firm and barely polite reply. Despite his apparent relaxed demeanour Tony was obviously still smarting from our experiences at the station. "No, we stay. Comprenez vous, mademoiselle?" Why a Welshman with an equal command of both the Welsh and English language should lapse into French to aid understanding between him and a Bulgarian, I could not imagine. For her part the young woman looked crestfallen as well as lost for words. I surmised she was trying to form a response in Italian or Spanish. In the end she chose English. "You must pay because I finish now. Understand?" Tony didn't, but slowly I was realising what was going on. The girl was obviously working on a commission only basis and needed to submit her takings to be paid. We had to pay her, but were welcome to stay and continue ordering from her replacement. I paid the young lady; she thanked me and once Tony was in conversation with her equally beautiful colleague he seemed to settle down too.

After an enjoyable evening we decided it was time to reclaim our bags and await the arrival of our train. We had enjoyed a few beers and were in mellow mood when we arrived at the luggage office. However, a more anxious mood overtook us when I tried to extract the luggage tickets from my wallet and discovered that they had completely disintegrated. We approached the dingy room wondering what response we would get. As so often in Bulgaria what happened next was not what we anticipated. With no reference to the need to show a ticket the luggage commandant made a sweeping gesture to indicate the bags under his command and invited us to remove ours. Luckily the pile of bags was small and locating ours was relatively straightforward. The guy would not have turned a hair if we had removed all of them.

So, bags in hand, we headed for the platform. There was still fifty minutes to departure, but our train was already standing in readiness for the journey. And who do you think was there to greet us? Yes, our obsequious little friend that had helped us, and helped himself earlier that afternoon. Tony's greeting was less than affectionate. "What the **** do you want? You've had your money now sling your hook!" I am not sure that the chap was familiar with this latter phrase, but the general tenor of Tony's statement was clear. Despite this he seemed at first determined to remain, until catching a glimpse of Tony's hardening expression he suddenly thought better of it, a positive move in the long and arduous process of improving East – West relations.

So we now bravely approached the train without any native assistance. The guard stood by the entrance to the carriage and almost bowed as we prepared to get on board. We did not know it then, but we soon learned that Bulgarians could spot a Westerner, a potential meal ticket, a mile off and they believe every one of us to be extremely wealthy. Hence the bowing and scraping as we approached. Perhaps Tony was already catching on and had decided to turn it to our advantage. As we passed the guard Tony pressed a note into his palm. They exchanged knowing looks and with not a word spoken we stepped aboard the train.

It was now dark outside and in the unlit station I had not been able to make any accurate observations about the train itself. Now that I was on board it looked strangely familiar. There was a good reason for this. The carriage we had entered was an old "Bundesbahn" (German Rail) model from the late sixties/early seventies the like of which I had travelled on through Germany many times as a young man. This was not conjecture on my part. None of the signage had been altered since the old stock had been purchased from Germany. I noted with some amusement that all the safety notices were still in German, helpful to me as a German speaker, but of little use to the native travellers. I could see that if an emergency arose I may well have a pivotal role to play!

We consulted our tickets as best we could, given that they were printed in Bulgaria's Cyrillic script, and relying on our ability to at least understand the numbers soon found our compartment. As we entered we were impressed to say the least. We were confronted by three bunk beds all with crisply ironed fresh sheets and three comfortable seats opposite them. It was good to see that the Bulgarians were keeping up the standards set by the original German custodians of the train and its rolling stock. Of course we were able to deduce that if the train were full we should expect a third passenger to share our compartment. We were a little disappointed about this, but nothing could alter the buoyant mood we were in. We had had quite a lot to drink, but we could both handle our ale and we had eaten a substantial amount too. So our mood was in no way alcohol fuelled. No, we were excited about our adventure and had become intoxicated by the experience rather than the beer. We were smiling like Cheshire cats and thoroughly looking forward to the journey when we heard footsteps approaching accompanied by a tap–tap sound. We formed various theories about the source of this, the most popular explanation being that Long John Silver was set to join us. Soon enough the mystery was solved. The door opened and a young blind man appeared before us, feeling his way into the compartment with his white cane.

I immediately went into solicitous social work mode, while Tony suggested that no exceptions could be made and that last in got the top bunk. I never ascertained whether he was serious about this because I had no sooner welcomed the guy and introduced ourselves when the door opened again, this time to reveal a middle aged Bulgarian already in his jimjams and clutching an old fashioned hard leather brown suitcase. He seemed bewildered and immediately the reason for this became clear. The guard stood behind him herding him into our compartment and as he reluctantly complied the guard indicated to Tony and me that we should move next door from where the unfortunate pyjama clad Bulgarian had apparently been forcibly removed.

We now found ourselves in a first class twin bed compartment of the highest quality. As a final confirmation of what had happened a pair of black shoes poked out from under the bottom bunk, presumably the property of the barefoot passenger who now occupied our old room. I glanced over at Tony who looked like the cat who had got the cream. "How much did you give that guard?" I asked incredulous and a little worried about the flagrant misuse of our limited resources. Tony counted on his fingers, silently mouthing the calculation. He opened a beer, leaned back in his chair and expertly poured it into the tilted glass that he had liberated from the last bar. "One pound sixty six pence." was his triumphant reply.

20014: Making Progress; Europe through New Eyes

Monday 31st March 2014: Beek, Holland to Köln, Germany

After yesterday's ordeal today was going to be a lot easier. Given the time I went to bed it was quite remarkable that by seven thirty I felt fresh and ready for the day. Particularly surprising given I could hear horses being loaded and unloaded most of the night and early morning. Given we only had about one hundred miles to travel today we took our time with everything.

When we were ready to go I went and asked the women in the office if we needed to muck out. Two old guys had been bustling about with wheelbarrows all morning so I was hopeful. "No, don't worry the guys will do it." was the welcome reply. It never ceases to amaze me how virtually every Dutch person speaks English almost like a first language.

For the second day running Flo was a nightmare loading. After all the training she is behaving like she has never been in the horsebox. We must of course remember she is only a baby and it all represents so much change for her. We held our nerve and our temper – stress down, success up as Monty Roberts, the horse guru, would say – and finally succeeded by putting Guinness in first.

We had a fairly relaxed journey through what is for us familiar territory. How well I know this part of the German motorway system from 40 years ago when I hitch hiked through it about 4 times a year, unable to bear more than a few months apart from Marieluise. Later when she had moved to Britain we did it together for years, the only way we could afford to regularly visit her family. On this journey we stopped at the service area known as "Rasthof Frechen", always a regular stopping off point for me in the past. It brought back many memories.

One in particular was where I had told a driver I wanted to be dropped off at Köln. I t was my normal pattern to name a town and then as we got closer to ask to be dropped at the next services. I had been getting on really well with this guy and we had talked about all sorts of things. Then about 3 miles before Frechen he decided to tell me he was gay and how it was easier to come out to a relative stranger who seemed like the sort of person who would give him a fair hearing. Remember this was 40 years ago. I immediately felt a shocking dilemma. He thought he was dropping me off in the town about 25 miles away and I was about to tell him I wanted to get out in about 2 minutes. It was clear that he would think that what he had said had caused me to flee. I stayed in the car for the next half an hour letting him drop me off at a place where I was likely to be marooned for hours, and so it proved. Was this the moment when I realised I was destined to become a social worker!

So after an uneventful journey – the type I like- we arrived at our destination in the hills near to Köln. It was a stunning setting.

Just a note here to say that every 2-3 hours on each journey we stop and give the horses water. What a pantomime! You have to push your way past their hay nets, entering from the living area, with a full bucket of water with each of them stretching their necks to get a suck. It reminds me of my brother Roy and me trying to get our lips 'round the first pint after a warm day at the cricket. Because he is the nearest Guinness gets first slurp and then as you pass on to Flo in a crouched position he proceeds to smack his lips dropping about a pint of water down your neck. Flo's habit is first of all to put her whole head in the bucket and give an almighty swish of the head. The result is that you get completely soaked from head to foot. She then puts her head back in and slowly drains the bucket in a way any bitter drinker would be proud of, with a series of almighty sucks. You have to love them to endure it. Luckily we do.

So back to our arrival at the yard near Köln. The road to the yard was stressful by lorry, about fifteen miles of tiny, bendy and hilly roads that seemed to go on forever. When we reached our destination it was worth all the angst, set in absolutely breath-taking countryside.

The horses were given a grassy paddock and had their heads down munching in a few minutes. It is lovely to watch them when they arrive at somewhere new. They look about a bit, circle the area, check out with each other and then start grazing. It is amazing how close they are becoming, almost literally. When at rest they stand within a few feet of each other and as each new experience presents itself Flo looks to Guinness, ten years her senior for reassurance that it is OK. When he then relaxes she takes her lead from him.

Sylvia, the proprietor, was a well-built healthy looking classic outdoor woman. At first sight I thought she was our age, but sitting down chatting I realised she was more like late forties. She could not do enough for us, making us coffee on arrival with the promise of breakfast before we left. Sylvia is a real animal person surrounded by horses, dogs, cats and chickens. She even dog-sits some neighbours' pets, including a nearly blind terrier who wears a high visibility jacket to ensure visitors don't inadvertently run him over. It is wonderful how our Jack Russell, Bridget just mucked in with all of them including the chickens. I suppose she is feeling a bit displaced in terms of territory and so goes with the flow.

We were so shattered that we were in bed by eight in the evening local time. I set the alarm on the phone and must have fallen into a deep sleep. The phone then rang an hour later and I pressed the red button to turn off the alarm. However, I was seven hours too early. It was my brother Roy ringing and I cut him off. I was just getting settled again when Marieluise came down the ladder from the top bunk. She too thought it was morning and was about to make tea.

An hour later the phone went again. This time it was our youngest daughter, Lucy. As soon as I said we were fine she burst into tears. I had promised to ring her and with going to bed so early I had forgotten. The poor thing was so wound up. I felt awful and again realised that friends and particularly family are living every minute and their anxiety levels are similar to ours before we set off. We, however, are getting more and more relaxed, because we are just doing it and it is no big deal

Tuesday 1st April 2014: Through Germany: Köln, to Nuremberg, Bavaria

Got up early again, about five thirty, made tea and ate some muesli. We then went into our now normal routine. The first thing is to check the horses are alright and are where they should be. Today we did it together as it was such a beautiful morning. They were happy and relaxed in the paddock. We fed them and then went back to the lorry and fed Bridget. The feeding completed we set about clearing all the "stuff" back into the living area, making room for the horses to go in the back. We had finished everything by seven and wanted to get going, but Sylvia had said she would have breakfast ready at seven thirty so we were forced to chill for a bit. This was good. We were making good time and there was no reason to shoot off. On such a mission it is hard to relax and neither of us is predisposed to relaxation anyway so waiting for breakfast was probably ideal. We just sat outside and took in the scenery. It was a truly beautiful morning with a cloudless sky promising a fair day ahead.

At seven thirty we sat down in a virtual banqueting hall together with Sylvia. She'd done a fabulous breakfast and we just relaxed and enjoyed her company. She seemed to enjoy having us there. For the first time we realised how interesting our adventure is to others. They ask us so much about the detail of what we are doing, as Sylvia did, what is our connection to Bulgaria and so on and soak it all up. I guess so many people say "One day I will do so and so", but we are actually doing it, so I suppose it is very interesting for people and they live a small part of it together with us. After breakfast Sylvia gave us a small picnic to take with us. I always say people are by nature kind hearted and this experience is proving me right.

So we got the horses and hey presto Flo walked straight into the lorry. Was this her finally accepting the whole thing or was it due to our relaxed demeanour. A bit of both I think and we had Sylvia to thank for the latter.

For the benefit of horsey people it is worth reflecting on some of the things we noted and learned about the way Sylvia organises her yard. Of course she runs a professional livery yard with about twenty horses and so is forced to consider how to make the job doable without wearing herself to a frazzle. Certainly there were some features of her yard that neither of us had seen before. For example most of the horses lived outside in a large enclosed area with an all-weather surface. Along one side there was a long row of walk-in feeding stalls which were part of an outbuilding adjoining the house. In this outbuilding, or annex was the feed and hay supply. So all you had to do to feed them was throw the hay into a bay in front of the feeding stall and they simply put their head over to eat it. During this whole operation you remain inside and whilst eating the horses are sheltered too. No carrying hay or filling hay nets, all dead easy.

So off again and after months of planning we enter day four in a perfect frame of mind and with everything on track. Travelling through Germany is of course made easier by the fact that we both speak the language. Also the motorways are excellent and the service areas give you what you need: decent food, clean toilets and inexpensive fuel. Funny to compare it to a British service area, which is a shopper/consumer experience, almost American style. Sometimes at home there seems to be more people at the services than on the road. In Germany they only stop for a quick snack, fill up and get going again. Consequently that is what the services gear themselves to. Also I have to ask why German motorway services manage to sell diesel for one Euro thirty five per litre, equivalent to about one pound fifteen. Anyway, for the time being I can stop getting excited about British prices.

So on we went, a long journey, but we were settling into it all now and we arrived unfazed at our destination at about four thirty in the afternoon. The yard we were staying at was in a delightful little village in deepest rural Bavaria. The yard was very small and catered largely for children's riding holidays. Marieluise immediately liked the place when she saw the sign for Aglashof, *Riding with the Heart*. The proprietor, Kerstin, was there to meet us in a state of excited anticipation. The area she had prepared for the horses was essentially a garage with a fenced off area in front of it. There was hay and bedding all ready for them so we put them straight in and they seemed fine. They were fine.

Kerstin was a funny little thing, slim and wiry. I put her at about thirty five, but we were later to learn that she was forty six. Soon we were introduced to "die Mama" who welcomed us with coffee and homemade cake at a ramshackle table amongst the melee of horses, cats and dogs. The oldest generation in traditional parts of Germany don't get to keep their Christian names and so soon an older guy came and introduced himself as "der Papa".

In essence Kerstin was running a serious riding holiday business from what amounted to a house with a large garden. Somehow it struck me like a riding centre as a child might envisage it and set it up in their imagination. This image in many ways fitted with Kerstin's youthful, almost little girl appearance. However, despite everything seeming chaotic, with everything on top of itself, it was a serious and well run business. Kerstin showed us to our own guest bathroom and toilet and we gratefully took our first shower since leaving home. For people who always take a shower or bath every day you would think four days is a long time without, but it is funny how you just get used to being filthy. Still, not knowing when the next opportunity would arise I even had a shave.

With the lorry cleaned out we took the horses for a walk in hand with Guinness pulling like a steam train. If he did that at home I would be really annoyed, but can you blame him after about ten hours in the wagon. When we returned die Mama called us for dinner, a traditional meal of potato pancakes and salad, followed by chocolate pudding with pears and cherries, both preserved by die Mama in glass jars from the last harvest.

I sat opposite der Papa and after a few niceties I asked him if he was born in the village. I was surprised to learn that he was actually from a town just outside Nuremburg, but had lived most of his adult life in the village whilst working in town. He had become a real devotee of country life and described his desperation to get back home to the village at the end of his working day. I could relate easily to this having worked for thirty nine years in Merseyside while living in rural North Wales.

Bavaria is renowned for right of centre politics, having never since the war elected Social Democrat administrations at any level of government. Imagine my surprise therefore when der Papa went into a passionate speech about the shortcomings of capitalism and the shocking effect on working men of being laid off by large multi-nationals. His views about the benefits of Socialism guaranteeing work were similar, even identical to those I have heard from East Germans and other Eastern Europeans that have found themselves on the wrong side of the Western dream. I was confused. What was his background? Had I misunderstood somewhere along the line? I was pondering this when my phone rang, I apologised to my hosts, but wanted to take the call as it was my brother Roy and I had not spoken to him since I cut him off the previous night mistaking him for an alarm clock. Roy shares my political perspectives as closely as anyone and he too was confused by der Papa's political treatise.

By the time the call was over der Papa had moved the conversation to the cosier subject of Bavarian beer, with the inevitable result. Der Papa informed me that in Bavaria half a litre was a small beer and a litre was a large one. With the beer standing there before me the inference was obvious: what are you man or mouse? I was grateful for the opportunity to show that the English can sometimes shape up and I also liked the look of the beer. So after draining the litre glass with the inevitable Schnapps chaser, downed in one, I was ready for bed. After a shower, die Mama's home cooking and der Papa's beer I slept with a smile on my face unconcerned at what day five may bring.

Wednesday 2nd April 2014: Nuremberg, Bavaria to near Vienna, Austria

Die Mama made us a traditional German breakfast minus the wurst and then some sandwiches to take with us made from what we couldn't eat at breakfast. She wanted to make us some coffee to take as well and was dumbfounded to learn that we did not have a thermos flask. Of course we had not had a Mama to help us plan the trip either. On reflection she is right, but with so much to think about the idea of a cosy coffee break between stops never really occurred to us. Instead we at least had an endless supply of water and juice.

Flo loaded like an angel and as usual Guinness walked into the wagon without even breaking stride. After kisses and hugs from die Mama and a generally emotional send-off within twenty minutes we were back on the motorway and heading for Austria. All went really well, the only hold up being at the border where we had to stop to buy Austrian road tax, known as a vignette at a cost of ninety Euros.

The Austrian accent took me by surprise. I went to buy the vignette expecting a normal conversation in German only to find that, although it was German he was speaking, it sounded like something else entirely. Each word is finished off so harshly that it sounded really weird to me. In fact he had to say nine<u>ty</u> Euros about four times before I finally understood, a process during which he displayed the patience with which the Teutonic race are naturally blessed, i.e. he went puce in the face and raised his voice several decibels at each repetition. I think that I thought nine<u>teen</u> Euros sounded more reasonable and so just kept hearing that. Not to worry we parted friends with our in-built prejudices about each other safely intact.

At about four that afternoon we left the motorway heading for our overnight lodgings. We were following signs to the village when Marieluise suddenly noticed a wooden sign to the left saying "Wiedenhof". I had already over shot and had to back up, but it did appear that we had found our overnight spot more by luck than design. Just to be sure Marieluise got on the phone and "Ursula" confirmed we were on track. We took the turning indicated by the wooden sign and as we had become accustomed to, headed upwards. After a difficult but mercifully short ascent we arrived at our destination. Ursula was there to meet us and after a long discussion about where to park we stayed on the road and unloaded the horses there. That went well and we led them to the paddock Ursula had set aside.

Ursula was so excited about the whole thing it was unreal. I mean *really* excited. By comparison I would describe Kerstin as laid back! She just wanted to do so much to help it was overwhelming. She offered to feed the horses for us; she offered us coffee; she offered us the use of her own bathroom; she said we could sleep in her guest room in the main house; she said we could take as much hay as we liked for the journey and then charged us only fifteen Euros all in! If Ursula, ever reads these next few lines, I hope she understands! She is one of the most generous people I have ever met, but what we wanted most of all was to see our horses settled, which she helped us achieve very swiftly, and then to eat something in our horsebox/home and get to bed. It is for this reason that we did not take up any of her offers with the exception of filling our four hay nets for the journey. However, it is the kindness and generosity of people on this trip that is making the biggest impression on us and we will remember Ursula with fondness for this reason.

Just as with Sylvia, Ursula had some incredibly innovative ideas to make looking after about twenty five horses relatively easy. The first thing to note is that almost all the horses there live as a herd. Why not? They are after all herd animals and so living altogether is completely natural for them. Observing them all in the field together confirmed that they had long since sorted out any hierarchy issues and they all seemed at ease with each other. It is ridiculous sometimes to see in British livery yards thirty or so horses divided from each other into small paddocks usually created by electric tape. It also makes the field look really ugly.

Stretching along one side of Ursula's large field was an enormous American barn. Each stall had an open back with a small individual enclosure protruding into the field as well as the usual front entrance into the barn. In the evening when they wanted to feed the horses and get them in for the night, they simply put the feed into each stall, opened the enclosures into the field and called them. Twenty five horses then came forward sorted themselves out with one horse to each stall and ate their evening feed. Ursula and her helper then went behind them and closed the gate of each enclosure. It was miraculous to watch. Once shut into their individual stall each horse could choose to stay under cover in the warm or take the air outside in their little enclosure. Some stayed in and others stood outside as suited them. Just like at Sylvia's, the supply of hard feed and hay was close at hand to make life as easy as possible. Watching all this I was forced to conclude that they have less hassle in feeding and bringing in twenty five horses than we have at home with three. It is great to be able to witness how others do things and learn from it.

By the end of the evening there was not a single person on or visiting Ursula's yard who had not been told about our adventure and her admiration for what we were doing was wholly genuine. As we continue on our trek we become more and more determined to find a way to respond positively to people's interest whilst at the same time remaining equally determined not to become overrun by this. We still have a long way to go and soon we will be leaving the relative comfort of Western Europe and all it has to offer. We must conserve our strength and remain focussed. We have three much loved animals with us who did not ask to be driven three and a half thousand kilometres across Europe. We must remain on top of things for their sake primarily and that means staying completely on track, following the plans we have made. We have planned this trip with military precision and we know what we are doing and what we need from people. So far at least we are making a good job of things.

In this context it is becoming a recurring theme one this trip that people who have never driven a 7.5 tonne lorry, let alone with two horses in the back, nevertheless put themselves forward as experts on whether I can or can't reverse the lorry or turn it round in the space available, where I will or won't be able to park and whether I will or won't get stuck on a particular surface. I am no expert myself, but as one day stretches into another I am certainly getting to know the vehicle and given the very rural locations at which we are staying I have already faced some difficult manoeuvres. I am becoming quite thick skinned with regard to this "help" and firmly make my own decisions which are proving to be correct. If a seasoned truck driver offers advice I will listen, but so far I have been the one best placed to decide what is sensible and possible. The same thing applies on the road. I know what feels like a safe speed with two horses on board and if that does not suit the driver behind me, tough.

Because we are determined to do things our way, we were again in bed by eight. When we wake up tomorrow we want to be fresh and I think we will be. I must admit though, it took me some time to get to sleep tonight. The day after tomorrow we enter Romania and everyone we have consulted has told us not to stop there. To our mind though, it is simply too far for the horses to travel without a stop. Adding to the anxiety is the fact that our overnight stop in Romania has been organised by a friend of a Romanian colleague who I know through my international work with Barnardo's. Neither Daniel nor his friend knows anything about horses as far as I am aware and the friend, Bran, has been very economical in communicating his plans. We will just have to hope for the best and trust our luck holds. Anyway before that we have Hungary to cross. Let's deal with that first.

2004: Early Discovery; First Impressions

4ᵗʰ April 2004

I am not sure what time we went to bed, but such was our excitement and anticipation we were awake at six thirty, bright eyed and bushy tailed. Although not due in Varna until eight o clock, the train was already slowing down for its arrival, or had it only been going this fast all night? It was hard to tell. Unconcerned we decided to go in search of breakfast. We searched and we searched and we searched some more. It would appear that the only carriage they had omitted to buy from the German Bundesbahn was the buffet car. This was a sleeper and apparently all you were supposed to do was sleep. Everyone else on board seemed to know this as we were the only people on the train who were out of bed. However, nothing could knock us and we simply returned to our compartment to await arrival. We would have breakfast in Varna.

We had chosen Varna as our destination because this was the main city on the Black Sea coast. From Varna we could strike out and visit all the Black Sea towns and resorts we had been reading about, Balchik, Kavarna, Obzor as well as the now flourishing holiday destinations, Golden Sands and Albena. We also wanted to explore Varna itself as we had heard it was a lovely city. However, as we trundled through the outskirts this positive view of the city was far from confirmed as we passed endless grey and listless high rise apartments, disused factories and miscellaneous derelict buildings. As we approached the centre of town things picked up a bit and our mood of optimism returned.

At exactly eight o clock our train shuddered to a halt in Varna station and we alighted with our cases ready to face the day. The weather was glorious. The station was more open and less dismal than Sofia and we found our way out easily enough. Almost directly in front of us was a large pavement café and we headed there. Tony had some sort of mixed sausage grill affair and I more conservatively had a plain omelette and toast. We both had several cups of coffee. I was fast discovering that Bulgaria was a good country for vegetarians, which I hadn't expected and we were both discovering that eating in bars and cafes was not going to break the bank. The total bill for the two of us was less than two pounds!

Breakfast over we set about looking for a hotel. Again we did not have far to look. Just across from us was a building with a frontage lit up in florid green and above it the sign announced that it was a high class hotel. We picked up our cases and made our way across the square. Not just the frontage glowed green, the same lighting arrangement adorned the reception area giving the impression that the young receptionist had appeared in a puff of green smoke like a genie. We half expected her to offer us three wishes, but she remained silent allowing us to state our business. We had no idea what the normal cost of a hotel room was so when she quoted their price for a twin room with breakfast we had no way of judging whether this was competitive or not. Given this we decided to book for one night only. We went up to our room and dumped our cases. We each had a quick shower in the inevitably green lit bathroom, passed through reception stopping only for basic directions, stepped back out into the beautiful sunshine and headed for the centre.

We spent the whole day in Varna city centre and can confirm that it is indeed an attractive place. The centre is built around a large pedestrian square with a huge fountain in the middle. It is full of small bars and cafes and individual small shops. There are random traders all over the pavement usually with no identifiable market stall, rather just a table or with their wares on the floor. They range from small clothes retailers usually with just one or two lines like jeans and tee shirts to old ladies with an old Salter bathroom scales offering to tell you your weight for a few pence. They were of dubious accuracy and when I rang Marieluise later that night I was able to give here the good news that I had lost four stone! There appeared to be only one department store and on closer investigation this turned out to house individual retailers and so was more of a shopping mall than a department store.

The most striking thing was that hardly any sales were being made anywhere. If you appeared to actually want an item about four members of staff combined to make the sale. Marieluise had requested that I try and find a Russian style woollen hat as modelled by Julie Christie in Dr Zhivago and after trying at several shops I found one. I enquired about sizes and realised I had indeed found one – the only one. I was however assured by a middle aged assistant with a fat head and a sylph like twenty year old that it would definitely fit my wife. They demonstrated the versatility of the garment by each putting it on their head although I discouraged the older lady from keeping it on for more than a few seconds in the fear that if it ever had been Marieluise's size it would soon be stretched beyond recall. I made the purchase and offered a note just one or two leva above the price. There then followed a pantomime that we were to see repeated time and time again. They had no change and were immediately thrown into a panic lest the sale be lost. Mind you once the older woman had the note in her hand she was not going to risk returning it and clutching the note to her person she set off on a tour of other retailers until the change she needed had been assembled. I left triumphant with my mission fulfilled while the two shop assistants sat down and lit up, wanting to relax and savour the rare moment of a sale.

Just an hour or so later I was to experience an even greater dedication to making a sale. I entered a tiny tobacconist to see if I could get some Silk Cut cigarettes for Marieluise at the local price. Once inside there was barely room for me and the shopkeeper. The woman did not sell Silk Cut, but when I mentioned that I wanted four hundred my fate was sealed. "Moment!" she said and before I knew what was happening she had locked me in and gone in search of the brand I had requested. Tony, waiting outside saw the whole thing unfold, including the turning of the key and the woman running off at high speed. He put his mouth to the letterbox and enquired after my health. When I gave a strangled and bewildered reply he was most reassuring. "Don't worry", he said, "she likes the look of you and has gone to find a vicar and a couple of witnesses."

I stood there not quite knowing what to think or how to behave whilst Tony suggested more and more bizarre explanations including the possibility that I was to be transported to Turkey as a slave. He himself dismissed that one however on the basis that he could not think what I would be any use for. Just then I heard a rustling from the corner of the tiny room and realised I was not alone after all. Crouched on a low stool pressed against the wall was a wizened old crone clad in widow's weeds. She looked up from the colander of peas that she was shelling and gave a toothless grin. "You want cigarettes – she get plenty", she imparted and returned to her work. Ten minutes later I was relieved to hear the key turning in the lock. The woman entered holding the cigarettes aloft in triumph. She handed me the goods and when I converted the price she was charging it worked out at about one pound, twenty five for twenty, so putting aside my temporary imprisonment the whole episode ended well.

By the end of the day we had the lay of the land. We knew of a few options where we could eat; we knew where most of the estate agents were situated and we had seen a reasonable looking hotel just round the corner from the where we were currently staying advertising rooms at less than half the price we were paying. We resolved to check out the next morning and make our way to the other hotel. Now it was evening and we were yet to make the discovery that would define our stay. The big question to resolve was where were we going to do our drinking? During the course of the day we had noticed some smart bars in the city centre and so after a quick shower we headed back in that direction.

As we passed through some run down streets we noticed a basement bar from which some shocking music and exceedingly loud conversation was emanating. From the outside it had little to recommend it. The sign was so bleached by the sun that the name of the bar could not be deciphered. The paint was peeling off the walls and some rusty metal steps led down to a battered front door that looked as if it had been witness to and also the primary victim of a number of drunken brawls. There were some lovely bars in the centre, but somehow this place arrested our progress throwing out a challenge to us. "Don't be ridiculous", I said. "The place is a hovel." "No, you're right", came Tony's reply. "We promised ourselves a great evening. There are some really nice places up in town." We started to walk off, but catching each other's eye we exchanged wry smiles. There was a moment's hesitation and then down the stairs we went.

The place had been buzzing with conversation, but the moment we entered it fell silent. Even the song on the jukebox seemed to come to an abrupt end. All eyes were on us: not just strangers but foreign strangers. We made our way through the cordon of silence and sat at the only free table. Tony, always bolder than me, greeted the assembled gathering. "Dobŭr den." He offered in a louder voice than was really necessary. Some customers gave a mumbled reply, but the staring and general silence was maintained. We took our seats and the landlord approached to take our order. "Dve biri, molya." I asked for two beers and broke with Bulgarian tradition by adding a "please" of which Tony strongly disapproved. The landlord went to the fridge and returned with two bottles of Dutch Amstel. "Ne, Bulgarish Bira – Zagorka". My response, although grammatically incorrect, seemed to hit the spot. A broad smile lit up the landlord's face and he deposited the two bottles of Amstel back on the bar with an air of contempt, returning with two bottles of Zagorka. With the demeanour of a schoolteacher rewarding his brightest pupils he set the bottles and two glasses before us, poured a little into each glass and stood back. We understood and simultaneously we took a long draught of the ale. "Perfect!" Tony exclaimed. Almost at once everybody returned to their conversations and soon the place was humming again. We were in!

God knows how much Zagorka we drank that night and how much food we consumed, but the bill, although ridiculously cheap, was about a foot long. Half way through the evening we left for a short while to seek a phone box and ring home. I spoke so much rubbish and laughed so hysterically that Tony had to take the receiver from me and assure Marieluise that I had not had some kind of breakdown, but was merely excited. Leaving our wives anxious and bemused we returned for more and very welcome we were. Eventually we had to call it a day as the landlord reported that we had seen off his entire supply of Zagorka and he was not going to insult us by offering Amstel again. We staggered out and somehow made it back to the hotel. We found our room and flung ourselves gratefully into our cots, but not before, in an attempt to shut the curtains, I had brought the whole thing: curtain rail, pelmet and all down on top of us. We slept like heavenly angels, although possibly a little louder.

5th April 2004

Surprisingly, given the beer we had consumed the night before, we were up quite early. We did our best to reassemble the curtains etc. and backed away carefully. They looked fine, but it was clear that the next person to breathe on them would bring the whole thing crashing down. We were intent on making sure it would not be one of us. We went down to a forgettable breakfast and soon checked out. Cases in hand we decided to make the hotel we had seen yesterday our first visit. Finding no reception we entered the bar/café to be met by a young woman who turned out to be the receptionist, barmaid, chambermaid and any other role that needed to be filled. She confirmed that the price of a twin room was as advertised outside and we decided to check in. However, she liked to do things properly and insisted on showing us the room. This could easily have been a mistake. We followed her up uncovered wooden stairs to the third floor and were shown into a low dingy room. In the gloom we could make out two single beds of pre-war design. The floor was covered by a threadbare carpet and the drab colourless curtains were drawn. "Let's put a bit of light on the subject!" Tony exclaimed and crossing the room he opened the curtains. This action however made no difference to the light in the room as six inches from the window was a brick wall. Tony was unfazed. "Does the telly work?" he asked. "Of course" came the now familiar reply. "We'll take it." he said. Without the burden of hearing my opinion the deal was concluded. Tony dropped his bags, extracted mine from my reluctant fingers and taking the key from the girl as he passed proceeded down the stairs. Without a murmur of protest I followed him down and out onto the street.

Now, with our accommodation for the week secured, the business end of our trip was due to begin. We had come to look at properties and that is what we intended to do. We headed for an area close to the city centre where we had noticed most of the estate agents were located. Having said that they were not initially easy to spot. The remarkable thing that they had in common was that they displayed almost no details of properties that they had for sale. They had signs in English and Bulgarian proclaiming their identity as estate agents – the preferred translation was "real estate office" – but they had nothing else in the window to support this proclamation. We entered what seemed to be the main branch of an estate agent chain.

We were initially greeted with considerable politeness, shown to a seat and told that the manager would be with us shortly. Within five minutes the manager, a woman in her mid-forties with close cropped red hair and a serious demeanour, appeared as promised and there the convivial atmosphere ended. We were given a very detailed rundown of the agency rules including the deposits we would have to pay, the limits on the service that could be provided and the circumstances under which we would forfeit any funds we had already paid. At no time were we asked what we wanted or what type of property we were looking for. We very politely advised her to rethink her approach and declined to do business with her. The biggest shock was that she seemed surprised. In explanation she told us that they were spending a lot of time showing properties to people who did not buy them, but when we indicated that this was normal for estate agents she seemed confused. She would not relax her rules and so we left thinking this was going to be harder than we had realised.

The next place we tried was from the outside more forbidding. There was a huge oak door with a relatively small sign saying "Bulgarian Real Estate". I tried the door, but it was locked. I then noticed a bell with an intercom. I pressed the bell and a deep voice answered in Bulgarian, presumably asking us to state our business. "We are interested in property." I said in reply to the unknown question. Without further reply there was a buzzing sound and this time the door opened. We tentatively entered and as we did so the door closed behind us with a loud slam pitching us into virtual darkness. Once our eyes had acclimatised to the darkness we found ourselves in a spacious unfurnished hallway with large marble stairs leading God knows where. Boldly we climbed the stairs and on the next storey encountered a dark room off the landing with the door slightly ajar.

We went in to be met by a Bulgarian giant wearing a suit similar to the one my Dad wore when he was demobbed from the army. "I Ivan." He announced, "Welcome!" "Thank you," I replied. I looked around for some kind of clue to indicate we were indeed in an estate agency, but found nothing to confirm this. "We are looking for flats and houses in Varna. Can you help us?" "Of course." he said and pointed to an ancient horse-hair sofa indicating that we should sit down. We obediently complied and now found ourselves looking up at Ivan's face looming about six feet above us. We waited for further advice or instruction but all that we got was further confirmation of his name. "I Ivan." he repeated smiling down on us with a fatherly air.

After what seemed like hours, I enquired again about property. In response Ivan seemed to remember his script. "My Kollegin, she…." At this Ivan's enormous fingers did a reasonable impersonation of his colleague walking away. "At one o clock my Kollegin….." His giant fingers indicated his colleague's expected return. I consulted my watch. It was just gone eleven. The prospect of sitting on the horse-hair sofa for two or three hours with Ivan looming over us was not a happy one. Tony and I turned to each other and simultaneously we got to our feet. Tony looked at Ivan and found himself addressing the knot of his tie. "At two o clock we come back." he promised. Ivan's enormous arm gave a sweeping gesture of farewell. "Welcome and goodnight!" he replied and we made rapidly for the door with no intention of returning. The prospect of actually viewing some properties seemed to be fast receding. Perhaps it was time for an early lunch.

In the afternoon we fared better. After much searching, we finally came across a professional estate agency, Address, and a pleasant and competent agent, Georgi Koev, with whom we were to form a partnership that lasted for several years.

Georgi Koev

6th April 2004

Today we hired a car with the intention of travelling as far along the Black sea coast as possible looking at the towns where we had seen a significant number of properties advertised on the net. The car we hired was cheap, but then it had already done nearly two hundred thousand kilometres. We rented it from a small independent holiday company and I suspect that it was a private vehicle belonging to one of the two women that ran and owned the company. I base this on the fact that we went into their office yesterday to ask where we could hire a car and there was nothing to indicate that they did car rentals. There was a pause, then a rapid exchange in Bulgarian before they announced that they could do it for us. Tony asked to see the car and it was the one parked immediately outside the office that they had undoubtedly travelled to work in. Still you should always reward enterprise and we agreed. Today the lack of any printed contract rather confirmed my belief. Were we bothered? Not really, we were beginning to understand how things work here and were determined to go with the flow and not expect everything to be "proper".

"Where are you going today?" the younger woman inquired. "We are travelling along the coast, firstly going north. We thought we might start with Balchik." Tony informed her. We had seen references to Balchik on the net described as a well-established cultural resort. "Oh, Balchik is so beautiful." She cooed. We do sightseeing trips there which are very popular. You must visit the old harbour. You will love it!" We thanked them both for their service and their recommendation, climbed into the "hire car" and departed feeling confident that we had made the right choice for our first stop.

It only took about three quarters of an hour to reach Balchik. Although the main coast road was relatively narrow and barely maintained there were very few cars on the road and so we could make reasonable progress. We did not quite know what to expect, but nothing could have prepared us for the dismal, decayed town that we drove into. "This can't be it!" I protested as the first buildings indicated that we were driving into a small town. "Well there's a bloody great big sign saying Welcome to Balchik in English and Bulgarian that disagrees with you." said Tony. Indeed before our eyes was a lavishly decorated sign proclaiming our entry into the resort. "They spent so much on the sign there must have been nothing left for the town itself." suggested Tony. However, it was clear that the lack of spending on the town long preceded the erection of the welcome sign.

Surrounding the town centre were numerous low rise apartment blocks that at first sight looked condemned and abandoned, but on closer scrutiny we realised that they were all still occupied. Some of the apartment blocks were virtually cleft in two with huge cracks through the middle of the buildings right from top to bottom so that the two sides of the building each leaned inwards. In one case the crack went right through the middle of some poor tenant's balcony so that the two sides of the balcony met in a sort of ragged V-shape and the balustrade was hanging in tatters. However, even this flat was occupied and the washing hanging on the balcony testified that the family still ventured outside.

We drove on and parked in the run down town centre with the intention of having an early lunch. No one could accuse Tony or me of being pretentious or fussy, but we could not find a bar, café or restaurant where we would consider ordering food. In the end we opted to buy bread and cheese from a small local shop with the intention of making our own sandwiches. I have no idea what had been used in the baking of the bread, but it was foul. It was not stale, more wet as if too much liquid had been mixed with the flour. It is hard to describe, but it was the first bread that I had tried in my life that was completely inedible. The cheese was no better. It felt like soft rubber and we decided not to find out whether it also tasted like it. The whole sorry mess was pitched into a nearby bin and we returned to the car. "Let's get out of here." said Tony, but I was not yet ready to write Balchik off. "What about the harbour?" I reminded him. "Yeh, what about it!" He already knew what to expect. I on the other hand was not ready to leave the place without visiting its main asset. Reluctantly Tony agreed and we followed the signs and the smell of the sea.

We soon arrived at the harbour. It was possibly more run down than the centre and seemed completely non-operational. On the horizon we could see two large metal ships that were so rusty as to make their original paintwork unidentifiable. They had undoubtedly sat there at the entrance to the harbour for decades. The few boats that were moored were derelict and often half submerged. The whole place stank of decay. By this time we were in need of a strong drink, but given our planned journey we decided we would have to make do with coffee. We looked around for a coffee bar or similar and found a clump of tables, chairs and umbrellas with a view of the harbour which we took to be a café, although there were no staff or customers to confirm this. We sat down and after a very short time a woman appeared from some distance away clutching menus. Her disappointment when we said we just wanted two coffees was palpable. Nevertheless, she ran off in the direction from which she had come and returned shortly with two coffees. To save her legs we paid for them immediately. The bill came to less than one lev. I gave her a two lev note and as usual she had no change. She was about to return to base again, but I could not stand to watch the poor sole running hither and thither and told her to keep the change. She was inordinately grateful and I am certain this was the only two leva that she earned that day. Time to move on.

From Balchik we moved on to Kavarna. On the internet we had seen a number of newly built houses that could almost be described as mansions. From the photographs they looked incredible. Most of them had four or five bedrooms with large outside terraces alongside a pool. They were ridiculously cheap and we thought well worth a look. Kavarna itself was another disappointment. The centre was dominated by a large Soviet style square where parades would have taken place during the Communist era, but now looked like an absurd relic of the past. The town and its people were shabby and lost. No positive adjustments had been made to the post-Communist present day and there appeared to be no tangible benefits from their country becoming independent.

The surprising thing was that when we found the houses that we had seen on the net they were as impressive as they appeared. Unfortunately they had been built in a town that was singularly unimpressive, one of those Bulgarian towns that will take decades to shake off its Communist past and not a town that has any hope of attracting new investment. As a final nail in the coffin the houses had been built only metres from a massive run down gypsy enclave, both depressing and intimidating. I have no doubt that the builders got the land very cheap, but this development was going nowhere. I would be surprised if they ever sold a single house.

Just for the sake of completeness Tony and I continued our journey north until the Romanian border, but we had seen nothing to suggest that we should be looking at this strip of the Black Sea for investment. We turned round and headed back towards Varna. On the way we stopped briefly to look at the two main resorts in this area, Albena and Golden Sands. These were large fairly new resorts that were now attracting quite a lot of British and some German tourists. Albena was quite well planned, whereas Golden Sands, built over a longer period was a mixture of older drab hotels and newer smarter hotels and apartment blocks. Likewise some of the bars and shops were well built and well presented, whereas others were quite shabby. In any event we had virtually decided from the outset that we would not sink any of our money into seaside apartments, given the tendency towards over building. Also there is the risk that a popular resort may just as a result of changing trends become unpopular. Neither of these risks are likely to apply to city apartments.

By this time we had decided that we would possibly not invest at all in Bulgaria, but if we did we would be looking at properties in Varna. It depended on what Georgi would be showing us over the next few days. Despite this we drove through Varna and headed south to look at two seaside towns that we had seen on the internet, Obzor and Byala. These two towns were about fifty kilometres from Varna and very close to each other and had at some time in their Communist past attracted tourists. The towns themselves were like a parody of fifties/sixties seaside haunts in Britain. They had some odd features like a small open air theatre built in the style of ancient Rome, but with a ghoulish psychedelic décor; a large paved area in which the paving stones had been painted alternately with black and white gloss; and a number of cafes with sixties style soft furnishings like screwed down red leatherette benches and walls painted black and purple.

The beaches were slightly away from the town. To get to Byala beach we drove down a dusty track, parked on an overgrown patch of wasteland and from there ventured forth on foot taking directions from a three legged stray dog who appeared out of nowhere to offer himself as our guide. On arrival we were not disappointed. The beach was stunning and the sea majestic. We took a barefoot walk through the warm white sand enjoying the pleasure you get from an unspoilt beach with the smell of the sea and the sound of the gulls. It was inviting and we started to wonder what the place would be like in ten years' time and asked ourselves if we wanted to be part of it. It would be an understatement to say that I am more romantically inclined than Tony and I was reflecting on just how lovely the place would be with some tasteful development that left the beach unchanged, but more accessible. Tony was more realistic. "Whatever they do you can be sure they will make a mess of it. They'll probably build a dirty great prom with hotels and apartments almost at the water's edge. It will be popular for a while and then people will move on to the next new resort. You won't like it!"

Byala Beach 2004

I reflected on what he had said. "You're right. They will make a mess of it and I won't like it." Come on", said Tony "Let's have a look at the beach at Obzor, apparently the development there is already underway." "No, why upset ourselves for no reason. Let's get back to Varna and have a pint." And that is exactly what we did.

7-8th April 2004

Right away we had told Georgi that we had no intention of buying anything on this trip, but if he managed to show as a range of well-priced properties we would be coming back in the summer to make some significant investments. We said at once that we were not prepared to pay any deposits or make any contribution to the agency's costs for showing us around. The reward, if there was to be one would come on our next trip. In order to accommodate our wishes Georgi had to break almost all of the agency's rules, but he decided to put his faith in us and, wisely as it turned out, he put two days aside and spent all this time showing us the full range of properties that Address had to offer. However this process did not get off to a smooth start. Although we had told Georgi that we wanted to see a broad range of properties, after a few hours we had only been shown older flats and apartments. We had not been shown any newly built apartments nor for that matter had we seen any houses. Over lunch we asked Georgi why this was. At first he was cagey, but eventually we discovered the reason. In Bulgaria estate agents charge the seller and the buyer for their services and each agent has a set of properties that he or she is responsible for selling. In Georgi's case it was older city apartments. This meant that if he sold such a property to us he would get a proportion of both the seller's fee and the fee that we paid as buyers. If he sold any other type of property to us then the commission on the seller's fee will go to another agent.

Georgi was a bit sheepish to say the least, but we were quick to assure him that we did not hold him responsible. The fact was Bulgarian estate agents seemed to be operating a system that ensured that customers were shown those properties that suited their agent rather than those that they wanted to see. As far as we could make out agents like Georgi received no salary and were dependent solely on commission for their earnings. Therefore it was clear that they would behave in this way. Once we had sorted this out and told Georgi the bad news that if we were to buy apartments we would go for new builds then we started to make progress. It soon became clear that Address had cornered a great deal of the market in Varna and elsewhere and Georgi was able to show us new as well as used apartments in the city and on the coast and also a variety of small and large houses in the city and in the surrounding countryside. We ended the two days with a very good idea of the properties available to us should we choose to invest.

Having spent the best part of two days looking at properties we still had one more task to undertake. Before we left home we had decided that one of us would open a personal account at a local bank so that if we did come back looking to buy property we would be able to transfer money here. Walking around Varna we had noticed a very grand and beautiful building which on inspection we had discovered was a bank. This had made an impression on us and so there seemed no reason not to head there. We had been informed that this was now a large private retail bank that had derived from a state bank of the Communist period. That probably explained why it was housed in such a grand and imposing building.

Given what we were later to encounter in dealing with Bulgarian banks the process of opening a private account was, although long winded, relatively straightforward. Whilst queuing for the third and final time Tony picked up the dulcet tones of a Scouser ahead of us in the queue. "That doesn't sound like a Bulgarian accent." Tony called out and "Stan" turned round and grinned at him. "Not quite." He quipped and in his usual way Tony was soon deep in conversation. In any event it is never hard to get chatting with a Liverpudlian. Standing next to Stan was an astonishingly beautiful young woman who by nods and smiles indicated that she was with Stan. Suddenly noticing that Tony was speaking to him, but actually looking elsewhere Stan decided it was time to introduce her. "Oh, sorry lads, this is Rada, my solicitor. If you ever need one she is brilliant! Don't even consider using anyone else." At this point Rada stepped forward to shake hands and give a bit more detail about herself. She told us in perfect English that she had a few English clients who were interested in buying property and she would be happy to be engaged by us were we to require a solicitor. She gave us her address and a landline number and shortly afterwards she and Stan left the bank. We put the details of her office address safely away, not at that point knowing that she would become one of the most important people in our Bulgarian adventure.

We spent both evenings at the "Fox in Varna" as we had dubbed our newly found drinking hole, named after our local village pub in North Wales. Our evenings there were made more enjoyable through meeting an old chap who had worked during the communist period in East Germany and who spoke reasonable, though heavily accented German. As I am a fluent German speaker we were able to hold admittedly laboured conversations with the landlord and some of his regulars. Tony would ask a question in English, I would repeat it in German and then the 'interpreter' would relay it to the landlord in Bulgarian. He would reply, the interpreter would repeat the answer in German and finally I would give Tony the answer in English. Sometimes for his own amusement and to remind me that he too was bilingual, Tony would repeat it in Welsh.

By this stage in our trip we were eating as well as drinking in the Fox in Varna. We felt comfortable there and they knew that I did not eat meat. They did not understand this, but through the interpreter Tony informed the landlord and the cook that I only had half a stomach and had to be careful. This was news to me, but it settled the matter and I did not have to worry about being given meat, though I must say it was surprising that they never wondered how with only half a stomach I could still down a gallon of beer each night.

9th April 2004

Our week in Bulgaria had been a revelation, but now it was coming to a close. Today we were taking an internal flight from Varna to Sofia before flying home tomorrow. The flight was at one in the afternoon so we had a leisurely breakfast, checked out of the hotel and were at the airport at just after eleven. Varna is the second biggest airport in Bulgaria, but given the size of Sofia International we were not expecting much. Nevertheless we were still surprised to get there and find only nine passengers in the whole airport and that included us. As it turned out we were all due to board the same flight to Sofia and so the chit chat between passengers was more akin to what takes place at a doctor's surgery than at a city airport. Given the numbers you would have expected it to take only five to ten minutes to check in and get through security and passport control. However, we were not to be so lucky. Today had been chosen as a training day for new staff and the staff outnumbered the passengers by about five to one. It took more than an hour and so by the time the formalities were complete it should have been time to board the plane. That is when the first announcement came:

"We apologise for a delay of one hour due to circumstances beyond our control"

That was it: no further details were given. We waited for almost exactly an hour before the second announcement:

"We apologise for a *further* delay of one hour due to circumstances beyond our control"

Tony and I seemed to be the only ones who found the lack of information unacceptable and given that we had about fifty members of staff to choose from we decided to make some enquiries. Some people we asked either said they did not speak English or stated simply that they did not know the reason. Other responses varied from a stubborn refusal to give any information through to what appeared to be downright lies. Nobody seemed in any way inclined to tell the truth to the passengers or at least not to their British spokesmen. After two hours the third announcement was no surprise to anyone.

"We apologise for a further delay of *two* hours due to circumstances beyond our control."

We were feeling helpless and just to make matters worse we could hear the rumble of thunder in the distance. Surely this was the source of the delay and if so why on earth could passengers not be told?

In the time we had been waiting Tony and I had made a full tour of the airport and taken note of all the activity within the departure lounge and outside. There wasn't much. Outside there was a small ancient aircraft with a propeller that we assumed was a private plane. The whole time we had been waiting two mechanics had been crawling all over it trying in vain to get it to start. As usual Tony's humour was still intact. "I suppose things could be worse" he joked. "We could be travelling on that thing." Just at that moment the old plane roared into life and we along with a few other passengers gave a mock cheer.

About ten minutes later we got the announcement we had been waiting for. "Can all passengers for Sofia report for boarding? Boarding will commence in five minutes." By now the storm was getting serious and my schoolboy calculations based on the speed of light and of sound told me that it was also getting closer. So whatever had caused the delay it was not the weather.

The nine passengers duly complied and after an unnecessary delay during which we were all again required to show our passports and boarding cards we were shunted onto a bus for the eighty yard drive to our plane. In the relief and excitement of finally getting underway nobody had even looked out to see which plane we were catching, but less than a minute later we knew. After its short journey the bus pulled up alongside the single propeller craft that had for hours been the subject of so much attention.

To an almighty crack and rumble of thunder that would have been a suitable soundtrack to the film, Armageddon, the wary but now resigned passengers mounted the steps. When it was discovered that the steps were about a foot short of what was required to reach the door, nobody seemed phased and one by one they gratefully took the outstretched arm of the pilot to help them aboard. The scene inside did nothing to reassure us: A number of the seats were broken, some had no backs and a few were missing completely. The two air hostesses showed each of us to an intact seat and then quickly sat down and strapped themselves in. As the two young stewards crossed themselves and the rest of us said a silent prayer we took off into the eye of the storm.

Once we were properly in the air and despite the considerable turbulence, the air hostesses unstrapped themselves and sprang into action. One thrust a Styrofoam cup into our hands and her colleague followed up with an enormous urn of treacle coloured coffee. She poured it out whilst each passenger holding their cup as instructed with two hands tried to keep the cup under the stream of boiling liquid. After no more than two minutes and with mercifully few scolding incidents we all held a cup of hot coffee. As the two hostesses stumbled across the lurching aircraft and again pulled on their seatbelts the captain announced with great ceremony that due to the delay the coffee was on the house. Our visit to Bulgaria was ending with as much drama as it had begun.

2014: The Journey Unravels

Thursday 3rd April 2014: Vienna, Austria to Taltos Tanya, Hungary

Day six and we wake up at five feeling bonny: breakfast in the lorry, chores done, horses in without fuss, and underway at seven. We said goodbye to our lovely host and headed for Hungary.

I have an unusual, but strong link to Hungary from childhood although until today I had never been there. When the Hungarian uprising against their Communist rulers took place in 1956 I was five years old. In those days Britain had a proud record of opening its borders to refugees from oppression and a significant number of Hungarians came to Britain, including a fair few who arrived in my town where there was a small refugee centre. My Dad was a good old fashioned Labour Party man and trade unionist and he and his comrades had a rota for visiting the centre to offer help. I am still immensely proud of what happened next. When my father's turn came he was so overwhelmed with empathy for the people he met that he befriended a significant number of them, taking two of them home to live with us. Although it was my father that made the gesture, my mother took it on the chin without complaint.

One of them, Paul Puzsta, soon got on his feet and ended up making a life for himself in Britain as a successful and highly regarded chef in London. He married another Hungarian refugee, Rosa – they at least knew they had the same political perspective - and they both became lifelong friends of our family. Paul colluded in a scam with me many years later when I was trying to impress Marieluise on her first visit to Britain. I took her to a swanky restaurant in the West End where she was amazed to see the red carpet rolled out for us with the best food and wine she ever encountered before or since. Paul, who was of course Head Chef, did a great deal to help me win her affection that evening although I did my best to undo it by taking two hours to find where I had parked the car in an area that she had started to think was my natural stamping ground.

The other young man that my parents opened their home to was only seventeen, Paul Binder. The young Paul ended up living with us for years until driven by a shocking home sickness and a desperation to see his family he took the chance of returning. As far as I know my parents never heard from him again and it is hard to avoid the conclusion that he was not well received by the regime and met a sticky end, although my Dad could never accept that explanation. He preferred to think Paul was just a typical young bloke who once at home forgot about us. Needless to say my Dad never forgot about him.

So as we entered Hungary, passing through the border largely without incident, I felt nostalgia for a place I had never before visited. With regard to the ease of our continuing journey, I was pleased to note that the major routes were all motorway as they had been everywhere else. The first part of the country that we passed through was extremely flat, almost like Holland, but slowly this terrain gave way to a hillier region, beautiful and as far as I could tell quite sparsely populated. I commented to Marieluise as we drove just how beautiful Europe is. It has forest, mountains and at this time of year a wonderful spring lushness. In such an incredible world why do men fight and nations fall out. It makes no sense.

As we neared our destination the motorway suddenly gave way to a series of potholed roads reminiscent of a Welsh farmer's back yard. Also our destination, a riding holiday centre and livery yard, proved very elusive and on the terrible roads I had to perform two U-turns. However we eventually found it and we were very pleased with what we saw. Taltos Tanya had been highly recommended to us by British acquaintances that had made the trip before us and we are grateful to them for that. To our mind this was the perfect stopping off point for our journey. We were shown where to park, which was perfectly suitable and our horses were billeted in a fairly large sand paddock with lots of hay and water. The beautiful young Hungarian owner, a blond ice maiden, then approached us and discussed our needs in flawless German. I am sure she would have done just as well in English. We agreed that besides the parking and livery we would have a shower that evening and breakfast the next day and a supply of hay for our ongoing journey. She also provided us with some eggs and milk. She told us the price, very reasonable it was too, we paid and that was it. We then spent a relaxed evening there. The weather was gorgeous and all my hopes of a positive experience in Hungary were fulfilled.

After dinner I had a few beers and Marieluise drank a few glasses of wine. We slept well and my misgivings about Romania, now next on the agenda did not reoccur, at least not on that evening.

Friday 4ᵗʰ April 2014: Taltos Tanya, Hungary to Baile Herculane, Romania

We had a very nice breakfast served by a chubby employee in the guest dining room at seven and were on our way by seven thirty. Given the weather, I had been surprised to see that Marieluise had her woolly hat with her at breakfast, but on returning to the lorry she revealed that it contained a picnic created from the lavish breakfast table. As we were the only guests it is certain that what was left would have been thrown away or consumed by the overweight employee, but I still felt a bit uncomfortable. Still, Marieluise pointed out that the most difficult part of our journey lay ahead and now it was all about survival.

We again negotiated the narrow roads and potholes, but this time with the advantage of knowing where we were going. In no time at all we were back on the motorway and heading for the Romanian border. It wasn't very far and soon the signs for the border started to appear.

When we arrived, for the first time someone showed some interest in what we were carrying; too much interest in fact because the border guard told us to lower the ramp so he could see our livestock. Marieluise took charge at this point and politely refused saying that he could climb into the living area and see them from there. This, to our surprise he agreed to, but not before a lengthy argument with his colleague. Which one was advocating the lowering of the ramp and which was giving the contrary view I have no idea, because we had now surrendered the advantage of language. For all I know they may have been arguing about last night's football. Anyway it mattered not as sense prevailed and the guard accompanied me into the living area, and viewed the horses through the sliding door. We had horse passports, an export licence and health papers and assumed he would now look at these to see that they corresponded with our cargo. Not so, with a "Have a nice day!" he waved us on. Immediately his colleague shouted stop and a second argument broke out. I slowly inched forward and with resignation they let me pass. We were in. Or were we? After the border guards came the border police. This time a young policewoman decided that what our nerves required was being screamed at about the folly of bringing horses and a dog into Romania where they will be at best ill-treated and at worst eaten where they stand. Marieluise gave her an over sympathetic hearing and she ended by imploring us to return to Britain with as many Romanian dogs as we could find to give them a good home. We sort of tottered forward; I put the wagon into gear, hoping that was it, but no, I did not yet have a vignette, Romanian road tax. I drove a reasonable distant from the still excitable young policewoman and parked to get out and buy the vignette.

The young woman in the booth took the details of the truck and prepared the vignette. I then went to pay; pleased with myself that I had an ample amount of currency for each country we were passing through.

"That will be twenty Euros", she said. "No, it's OK I said smugly I have plenty of Leu."

"I am sorry we only accept Euros, not Romanian money."

Had I dreamt the last thirty minutes of passing through the border or, worse still, was it just a practice run. "I am now in Romania, aren't I?" I enquired. "Of course" was the definitive reply. So back to the wagon I went to get Euros to pay a Romanian civil servant who adamantly refused to accept the country's own legal currency. Strange!

We were now definitely in Romania. To my surprise we found ourselves on a brand new motorway that regularly announced that it was about five hundred kilometres to Bucharest. Could it be possible that this motorway would continue to the capital, which was exactly our direction? I dared to dream when suddenly after about twenty miles the motorway ended abruptly. I could see the unfinished road stretching before us still proclaiming Bucharest as its final destination. Typical that the road signs are in place although the motorway itself is still in an early stage of construction. We were shunted off onto a side road and in a very short time the roads deteriorated to an appalling condition. This whole thing reminded me of my first ever visit to Bulgaria ten years earlier. Then you often found yourself on brand new motorways started with European loans, but never more than twenty or thirty miles long, sometimes much less. Now in Bulgaria the roads are generally, although not always, much improved. In Romania they are apparently still full of potholes and I resigned myself to a long journey.

Although we were making slow progress, the weather was good and we were on course to reach our pre-arranged destination, Baile Herculane at about five which was fine. Then, crossing a mountain pass disaster struck; one of the rear tyres blew. Thank God the rear axle has two wheels on each side so I was able to limp on until I could find somewhere to pull over. Unfortunately, it was thirty miles before an opportunity presented itself. We stopped in a siding in a small village. While Marieluise got on the phone to the international rescue services that we had arranged, I got under the wagon and started putting into action what my mate, Richie had taught me.

Richard has a large plant hire firm with a number of lorries amongst his entourage of heavy machines. They do all their own servicing and before this journey started he and his son James, with my novice assistance, went over the wagon with a fine tooth comb. This included removing all the wheels, including the spare, and greasing everything before replacing them. This particular task he made me perform and was I grateful now. I have to admit, Rich, that it took me over two hours to get the spare on, but I did it. Bear in mind that I had to do it with two horses on board.

The whole time I was observed by two blokes and an old Baba sitting on a nearby bench. They never moved. In fact, there were times, brought on my heightened state of anxiety, when I thought they were statues; some Ceausescu inspired tribute to peasantry. Even their facial expressions were unchanging and so the matter was never definitively resolved one way or the other. Although the breakdown service was very communicative, with the Romanian operator impressing Marieluise with her English, no one actually appeared. So, now stressed beyond endurance and with no spare tyre, we were back on the road, or what Romanians call a road.

Now of course we were way behind schedule and heading for an unfamiliar destination with no real clue as to what type of accommodation awaited us and our horses. Although the quality of the roads improved they were extremely mountainous and so going remained slow. However, Marieluise did manage to raise our host Bran on the phone and let him know we would be late. It was all, as far as he was concerned, "No problem".

By the time we arrived at the town it was approaching six thirty and we were goosed. It seemed a long time ago when we had left the security of Taltos Tanya. Now we were parked up at the edge of the town waiting for Bran to come and meet us. About ten minutes after Marieluise had told Bran we had arrived, he appeared in a battered old car and told us to follow him. I tried to impress upon him that he would have to drive slowly to allow me to keep up with him. Bran was an odd looking guy with one eye apparently lost to a gruesome accident and shoulder length black hair. He did not inspire confidence, but what could I do but dutifully follow?

As expected he shot off like a bat out of hell with me doing my best to follow him without sacrificing the five lives on board. It was not easy and eventually I resigned myself to losing him. For a long time he was not in sight, but given all the options other than straight on were decidedly unappealing I just stayed on the road. After not seeing him for five minutes we finally caught up with him parked by a right fork. I looked up ahead to see a mountain looming before us.

"Well let's hope he doesn't mean us to go up there!" I said half in jest. It didn't take long to realise that was exactly what he did expect. I was now driving in second gear at crawling pace around hairpin bends and ever upwards. Again the man I loosely describe as our guide was soon out of sight. I was holding the steering wheel with an anxiety induced grip of iron. Surely this would not go on for long, we thought, but it was another ten minutes of driving purgatory before we spotted Bran again. This time he was standing in the road with his mobile clasped to his ear shouting and gesticulating, as we later discovered in earnest conversation with the man who was to be our host for the night, apparently it seemed with some reluctance.

Abruptly the conversation came to an end with Bran staring at his phone. With a cursory wave and a barely audible "Please follow" he was off again. As the journey continued it became apparent that we were passing through some sort of holiday resort from hell. The first indication was as we passed a semi-derelict fun fare of which the only remaining customers seemed to be three stray dogs, presumably feasting on the remains of some rotting nougat or candyfloss. Further up the hill we passed a lake with some ancient wooden beach huts alongside and a cluster of naked bathers, clutching for towels as we passed. There was no need as our instinct was to avert our eyes from this terrible sight. Yet another stray dog was relieving himself against one of the bathing huts out of which another human form emerged yarning, apparently woken by the sound of our wagon trundling by. On and ever upwards we went.

Eventually, after "following" Bran for about half an hour we reached his parked car and by a series of gestures and broken English he indicated that we had reached our final destination. We pulled up outside a large renovated house and were greeted by its owner, an old fellow with a permanent smile that left you feeling uneasy rather than welcome. It soon transpired that the house was a guest house and the chap proceeded to show me to our room. At this stage Marieluise had not emerged from the vehicle, more intent on ensuring that the horses hadn't suffered some kind of equine altitude sickness. I started to explain that we had accommodation for ourselves in the lorry, but I suddenly decided to give up on this. What did it matter? It was never going to cost a fortune so who cares. I did, however, as soon as possible enquire about the accommodation for the horses.

Given all the delays of the day – the burst tyre and then the mountain ascent – it was now getting dark. I was led into a sort of terraced garden adjoining a grassy slope covered in small trees. I assume it was some kind of orchard. You entered it through the main gate to the house and the parts I could see, alongside the road were fenced off. I asked if the whole plot was fenced and they assured me it was fenced on three sides and ran down to the banks of the lake on the fourth side. By this time Marieluise had joined me and was looking very wary about what we were being offered. In particular she did not like the fairly severe and rocky slope from the terraced garden where we stood down to the orchard. Mind you this was her concern based on what we could see. Before the night was out our concerns had turned to utter panic. It was now too dark to properly investigate the whole plot and the horses were making it known that they were fed up and wanting to get out of the lorry where they had now spent about twelve hours. We again asked for reassurances about the security of the fencing and decided that we would lead them down the rocky slope into the orchard and let them go. We got them out of the wagon and at this point Bran decided to make a hasty exit leaving us in the care of the smiling assassin. This unnerved us slightly, but the horses had seen and smelt the grass and were deciding the issue for us. We led them into the orchard and let them go. As it turned out this was the worst decision we had made thus far.

The old owner of our guest house now left us too. We were the only occupants. There were about six guest rooms each with en-suite bathroom and clean towels. In each room there was a large double bed and each bed was made ready for occupation; but by whom? We had not been given any keys to the house which was open as was every room. The old guy had not given us any instructions about the morning. He had however left a large very old dog as a sort of caretaker. He certainly wasn't interested in any guard duty. I know that Bram Stoker's Dracula is set in Transylvania which is part of Romania and my imagination was working overtime, but this was just like a scene from one of the old Hammer horror films when the couple arrives to such a place apparently ready to accept guests and is met by

Dracula's old retainer. The sun was now going down and the old retainer had left. The scene was set for Dracula's arrival. Instead a disaster of a different kind befell us.

The horses, so carefully and lovingly transported for nearly three thousand kilometres thus far, had disappeared. We searched the area belonging to the house and they were nowhere to be seen. We were frantic. With the aid of one headlight and the torch in my mobile we searched and searched, stumbling around in the darkness. We made two chilling discoveries. Firstly, the high fence on one side of the property was completely on the ground and beyond it a massive green pasture stretched as far as the eye could see. Secondly, it was true that the garden cum orchard was bordered on one side by a lake, but between the orchard and the lake was a sheer drop. I kept telling myself that horses are sensible and value their own survival, but anxiety was starting to get the better of me. Marieluise's anxiety was already at fever pitch, but however she felt she was going to carry on looking all night if need be. The situation was desperate. We could barely see. The terrain was difficult and dangerous. Given the altitude and the remoteness of the spot we had absolutely no signal on our phone. Anyway, who would we have called? Certainly not the two people who had put us in this position. We had no other option than to keep on looking and this we did in as organised a way as we could manage given the debilitating effects of acute anxiety. We searched for nearly three hours. And then suddenly they were there, almost back where they started by the house.

It was Marieluise who found them and when I arrived at the scene she had Guinness on a head collar and had used the rope she had to rig up a halter by which she was holding Flo. I don't think an earthquake would have induced her to let go, but as it happened they seemed relieved to have been found and when I got to them they were all three standing stock still and as quiet as mice. Not only were the horses in completely unknown territory, they had come during this long journey to view us as their comfort blanket and I genuinely believe that they were bereft without us as much as we were without them.

Now that we had found them we were taking no chances. It was now between eleven o clock and midnight. Almost without discussion we had decided they were going back into the horsebox forthwith. All the arguments about ensuring they do not spend too much time in the lorry, pale into insignificance against the imperative of keeping them safe. In the lorry they were safe and they must have agreed with us because they walked straight in without a backward glance. We made sure they had plenty of hay and water and in a short while they settled down, content to spend the night in familiar surroundings.

We had had nothing to eat or drink for hours, but that was no longer of interest. We each drank a glass of water and were wanting just to get a few hours' sleep and then to get the hell out of here. Marieluise went to sleep in Dracula's castle – death by a vampire bite would have been a merciful release at this point – and I squeezed into the horsebox amongst all the "stuff", unwilling to let the horses out of my sight. A terrible day had ended less terribly than we had at one time feared.

2004: The Pleasures and Pitfalls of Buying Property in Bulgaria

Tuesday 6ᵗʰ July 2004

When we returned home in April we were uncertain about what we should do next if anything. We had enjoyed ourselves immensely, but that did not mean that we should automatically invest hard earned money in Bulgarian property. We had collected a lot of information about the country and particularly about the property market. We had also taken many pictures which gave a flavour of the country as well as an accurate impression of what property could be purchased at what price. Looking at this information ourselves we concluded that it presented a very mixed picture. Bulgaria was a country emerging patchily from a long period of Communist rule. It was a very poor country. This much had been obvious to us, but was also confirmed by comparative data on European economies widely available on the net. The property we had seen was extremely cheap and the new builds were usually, but not always of a high standard. The question for us was whether the country would improve economically with house prices rising alongside. There were a number of negative factors: recent history, widespread corruption and stifling bureaucracy; but there were positives too. Particularly amongst young people we had found an overwhelming desire to modernise and to become part of Europe both economically and culturally. Overall we felt optimistic about their ability to do so, particularly if their attempts to join the EU were successful. Also at the end of the day there was an overriding failsafe: it was hard to imagine their property prices getting any lower. We were inclined to invest.

Before we left to visit Bulgaria in April we had talked in the pub and at work about our plans and people had shown some interest. When we got back we found that the levels of interest had increased significantly. Given that so many people wanted to know in detail what it was like we decided to do a brief presentation in the village hall to all interested parties. One of the potential benefits to us was to see what others thought of the enterprise thereby confirming or otherwise our inclination to invest. The response could not have been predicted. Not only did people feel positive about Bulgarian property, they wanted a slice of the action. After a repeat performance at a more upmarket venue – a local golf club – with a slicker presentation we found ourselves forming a loose mutual company, which we called Bulgaria Property Mutual, to accommodate the varying levels of investment that people wanted to make. All those interested were required to make a minimum investment of two thousand five hundred pounds which would constitute one share. Most people decided on either two or four shares, although a small number invested quite a lot more. In all we issued ninety two shares. Hence, what Tony and I always referred to as "the group" was formed.

The upshot is that we arrived this time, three months after our first visit, with a clear mandate to invest in Bulgarian property and the best part of a quarter of a million Euros to spend. Georgi would definitely be pleased to see us.

One thing I had promised myself was that our travel arrangements would not include any internal flights, but I need not have worried. In the short time since our last trip the options had improved greatly. Some of the British tour operators had started doing package tours to Bulgaria's Black Sea resorts and the best choice turned out to be a direct flight from Manchester to Varna with a hotel in Golden Sands. From this location we could make daily trips into Varna to undertake our business with some prospect of having some fun in the evening. As we walked out of the airport and got aboard our transfer bus for the short drive to Golden Sands we were feeling pretty pleased with ourselves. When we arrived at our newly refurbished hotel we were definitely pleased with ourselves. Our days of staying in the cheapest hotels were over, at least for now.

Wednesday 7th July 2004

We were staying in a quiet family hotel some distance from the main thoroughfares of the resort, but very handy for buses and taxis to Varna. This was really ideal for us and I congratulated Tony on his selection. He took the praise in his stride, so much so that I was left uncertain whether we were at this hotel through positive selection or plain good fortune. It did not really matter one way or the other, it suited us perfectly.

Despite the charm of the hotel, the pull of the shoreline and the beautiful weather, we were very focused and business-like. By nine o clock we were in a taxi on our way to a pre-arranged meeting with the Address estate agent, Georgi. After meeting Georgi in April we had not been in touch with him until a week ago when we sent an e-mail to make this appointment. We both liked Georgi a great deal and in particular we liked his straightforward honesty. "H, Guys! Good to see you. When I got your e-mail, it was a pleasant surprise. You had not been in touch and I did not really expect to see you again, but here you are, after all. Dobŭr den!" In return we greeted Georgi warmly – we were genuinely pleased to see him - and assured him of our best intentions. Without disclosing the amount of money at our disposal we told Georgi that we were now on a serious property buying trip.

Having discussed it at some length, Tony and I had decided that our biggest investment would be in newly built apartments in Varna and very soon we were travelling around with Georgi, by taxi, looking at what Address had in this line. After about two hours the three of us were dropped off at a large new apartment block that had just been completed, but was not yet occupied. We liked the look of it immediately. Georgi contacted the building firm's on-site representative and we were taken to see the show apartment. Unlike the others this flat already had the kitchen installed and was furnished to help the prospective buyer imagine what the finished place would look like. These were large three bedroom apartments and we were impressed. We asked to see one of the actual apartments that was still unsold.

Tony and I have both done a lot of the building work in our own homes, me renovating an old cottage and Tony building a new house, so we were both in a position to make informed judgements about the standard of building work. There was no doubt at all that these apartments were built to the highest standards and were also nicely finished. "Yes we'll take it." said Tony with a minimum of fuss that took Georgi and the representative by surprise. Just as they were regaining their equilibrium, Tony followed up with:" Is the flat below available?" The representative assured us that it was. "Would you like to see it?" Georgi enquired. "Is it the same as this one?'' asked Tony. " Yes, they are identical, but if you want the one below instead, that is no problem. We will go and look at it." said Georgi. "No need," said Tony. "We'll have it!" "You prefer the lower floor?" asked Georgi a little bewildered. "No, we'll take both of them." was Tony's straightforward reply. Georgi stared at him wordlessly, then at me for reassurance. I nodded my agreement and as I did so I could hear the cogs grinding in Georgi's brain calculating the commission on the sale of two newly built apartments.

Our first property purchase in Bulgaria: 2 apartments in this block

The firm's rep was the next to speak wanting to know the colour schemes we wanted for the bathroom and the floor tiles. I decided it was time for me to get in on the act, but I wanted to respond in the same vein as Tony. "Just make it all the same as the show house." I said. "And what about the apartment below?" she asked. "Just the same, exactly the same." was my firm reply. "If you going to be looking for tenants, let's just hope they do not become friends" said Georgi, trying to lighten the mood. "They might be surprised to see their apartments are absolutely identical!"

"Is that it then?" asked Tony, now becoming more interested in where we could get some lunch. "Not quite," said the rep. "I just need to ask you about the kitchen. Do you want our firm to install it or do you want to organise it yourselves? Our firm's price is four thousand Euros, supplied and fitted." Suddenly Tony forgot about lunch. "I beg your pardon?" The young lady fearing her English had not been up to the mark, repeated her question. "I'm sorry if there has been a misunderstanding." said Tony. "As my friend said, we want everything exactly the same as the show apartment including the kitchen, but there will be no extra cost." She looked alarmed and surprised. "I will ask my boss, but I do not think this will be possible." "There is no question to be asked," I interjected. "If he wants to sell two properties right now then we want fitted kitchens in the price, simple as that!" She remained non-committal. "I will call him and ask." At this moment Georgi could see his biggest ever commission disappearing before his eyes. His intervention was swift and assertive. "I will call him." he decreed and within seconds his phone was pressed to his ear. Less than a minute later following a rapid exchange in Bulgarian he put his phone back in his pocket. "It is agreed!" he exclaimed at which Tony shook his hand and turning to the bemused rep did likewise. "Time for some lunch!"

After lunch Georgi wanted us to come back to the office for the formalities no doubt wanting to secure his sale, but we had had enough by then and made an arrangement to see him the following morning. He looked crestfallen, but we assured him that we would be there in the morning to tie everything up and off he went. Anyway, from our point of view this was now getting serious and before we did anything else we needed to find a solicitor. We were both reminded of meeting the Scouser, Stan, in the bank during our last visit accompanied by his beautiful solicitor, Rada. Tony opened his little note book that he had carried everywhere during our two trips and triumphantly produced Rada's address and phone number.

We soon found a phone box. At that time in Bulgaria they were everywhere and all working. I dialled the number and got a tone indicating number unavailable. Perhaps I had misdialled, but I tried again carefully punching in each number, but each time with the same result. We had to face facts. Rada had not given us a mobile; we did not have any contact information regarding Stan, so all we had was an address written in Cyrillic script. This was not going to be easy, but we were driven on by Stan's glowing reference. "This is Rada, my solicitor. If you ever need one she is brilliant! Don't even consider using anyone else."

The first thing we did was buy a street map, but without even knowing the order of the Cyrillic alphabet it was hard to find the street, although we eventually did. The next issue was orientating our current location to our desired destination. It is difficult to describe how hard this is when every word you look at is just a jumble of unfamiliar letters. We couldn't even say the name of the street we were looking for. To cut a long story short we eventually found the street by accident. Completely lost and staggering aimlessly about we rounded a corner and there it was. The relief was palpable. In trepidation we approached number 16, but as we got closer there was no hiding from the fact that the building was empty. About to give up and head for the sanctuary of the Fox in Varna at the last minute we saw a scrap of paper pinned to the door. Trying not to get too excited we approached and tried in vain to read the message. It was impossible, but amidst the words that made no sense to us was a number, undoubtedly a phone number.

For the second time that afternoon we looked for and found a public call box. This time I dialled the number in the knowledge that we were now in the last chance saloon. The number started to ring and after no more than ten seconds what sounded like an older female voice answered in Bulgarian. "Rada Yordanova?" I ventured. "Moment." came the reply. There was a rustling sound and then the sound of someone picking up the phone. "This is Rada. Can I help you?" I explained who I was and referred to the meeting in the bank which she seemed to remember. "My new office is in Kranevo Street.

Do you know it?" I confessed that I did not, although it turned out that we were about one hundred yards from her office at the time. "Do you know the cathedral?" I was overjoyed to tell her that I did know it. "I will meet you there in ten minutes. Is that OK?" I confirmed that it was very much OK. "In case you do not recognise me, I am wearing a camel coloured jacket." Ten minutes later we arrived at the cathedral and saw Rada standing on the steps. The information about the camel jacket was superfluous. She might as well have said, "Look out for the most beautiful woman in Varna. That will be me!"

Thursday 8th July 2004

As promised we got up early the next morning to head for Varna to meet Georgi. On the previous morning we had spent twenty minutes bargaining the taxi fare down from twenty leva to ten. As we approached the taxi rank this morning we spotted the same taxi driver. "I know, I know - ten leva." We smiled our agreement and from that day on we never paid more.

We had suggested to Rada that she accompany us to the Address estate agency office, but she already had an appointment. "Don't worry, if you are unsure about something just call me." We arrived just after nine o clock and this morning Georgi had reinforcements in the form of his manager, a smarmy looking man of about forty. After all the normal pleasantries and an assurance from the manager that we were making an excellent purchase we got down to business.

"The process is as follows: You must first of all pay a deposit to us to secure the purchase. This is of course taken off the final price when you settle the account. Georgi will then draw up a preliminary contract for you to sign. I will check it on your behalf..." "Just hold it there." I said. "We have a solicitor to check things for us and I also need to speak to her about this deposit." "Of course" he replied, "You can use our phone. What is the name of your solicitor?" "Rada Yordanova." I replied unaware of the response this would illicit. "Rada Yordanova from Kranevo Street?" "Yes, you know her then?" I had picked up the phone and Tony had handed me her new business card displaying her mobile number. "Just one moment please." said the smarmy manager and he took Georgi aside for a quick consultation. Then to our surprise he disappeared upstairs and it was Georgi that approached us, the extra authority of his manager now apparently unnecessary.

"There is no need to pay a deposit at this stage. I will talk with Rada about the preliminary contract and when she is happy with it we can all get together to discuss it and she will no doubt advise you from there. My manager has said this is how she likes to work." Tony smiled a knowing smile no doubt recalling Stan's recommendation. "That sounds very satisfactory." he affirmed. Georgi shook our hands and we headed for the door. "I will call her later today." he called after us. "Bye for now." Tony turned to me. "She may look angelic," he said, "But there is obviously more to her than meets the eye. She has changed the whole process and we haven't even consulted her yet!" By the end of this busy week that we had now embarked on Rada would have displayed her steely side on more than one occasion as well as demonstrating to us that she was indispensable to our project. We never met Stan again although we often enquired after him, but that chance meeting with him made a huge difference to our enterprise.

During lunch we did a short review of our current position. Despite two significant purchases we still had quite a lot of money to invest. Not on this trip, but at some point in the future we had promised ourselves that we would take a look at Veliko Tarnovo. This was a small city in central Bulgaria that at one time had been the country's capital. It was now famous as a city of education and culture. It attracted a great deal of tourists and was said to be very beautiful. It was also becoming popular as a destination for people interested in overseas property. However, even leaving aside money for possible investment in Veliko Tarnovo we still had enough for another property. Wanting to stick with our plan of investing in newly built city apartments we thought that we would ask Georgi to show us some one bedroom flats. "Well," said Tony, "there is no time like the present. Let's go back and see him now"

Ten minutes later we were back at Address and as George came down the stairs into reception he looked worried. "Georgi, why are you always so anxious?" I enquired. "The two apartments: that is a done deal. We are back because we still have some money left and want to look at some smaller apartments." Georgi was starting to think that meeting us was one of the best things that had happened to him and at that time in financial terms he was probably right. The interview areas were just off reception and each time we came to see Georgi looking for properties one of the receptionists seemed to take a particular interest in proceedings. I mentioned this to Georgi who smiled. "She always wants to know if I am doing well selling properties." He said. "Why is that," I asked. "She is my wife." he explained. "Well you better come up with something we like." Tony interjected. "Otherwise there will be hell to pay when you get home."

We spent a lot of time in the office that afternoon talking through the offers Georgi was coming up with. The reason we did not go looking at properties was because the best looking ones had not yet been built. Finally we came to what Georgi said would be ideal for us. These very chic looking one bedroom apartments were, according to Georgi, being built in the nicest suburb of Varna by the best builder he knew. We remained sceptical. It had never been our intention to buy off plan because of all the horror stories one hears about people losing their money on properties that never get built. However, when embarking on this venture we had told ourselves that we would find people we trusted and go from there. From the outset we had liked and trusted Georgi and on top of that we now had Rada to help protect our interests. Also we had confidence in our own common sense. We did not believe that we were the sort of people to get turned over and throughout this venture we had been the right combination of bold and careful.

I decided to be open with Georgi. "Georgi, we do not like the idea of buying off plan. If we do go ahead it will to a large extent be because we trust you." Georgi could not have given a better reply. "Thanks, guys, but let's be certain about this. We will first of all go and look at the site and then at some other apartments the same man has built and then you can decide." That is exactly what we did, but to all intents and purposes the decision had been made. Later that afternoon we confirmed the third purchase of our trip.

That evening, back at our hotel in Golden Sands we had a lot to celebrate. We decided that we would have a couple of pints in the hotel and then go into the resort, have a meal and see some Bulgarian nightlife. I decided to have a shower first and Tony went off to the bar. When I joined him fifteen minutes later he was cosily installed in a corner seat with his pint of Zagorka on the table in front of him. Since our early days at the Fox in Varna we had not drunk anything else. Tony had one of his mischievous grins on his face. "What is it? What are you grinning at?" I asked, not for a moment expecting a proper explanation. "Was I grinning? Well after the day we've had we should both be grinning all night." "I suppose you're right." I said, but there was more to it than that. Of this I was certain.

Just at that moment one of the senior members of staff walked by, but on seeing Tony he stopped. "Is there something I can get you gentlemen?" he asked. "A beer perhaps?"

"Yes, thank you; two Zagorkas would be perfect." The kind fellow went off to fill the order, but Tony wasn't finished yet. "Oh and two small Rakia would go down well." "I know we are celebrating, but it's a bit early for spirits isn't it?" I suggested. "Have something else then, Champagne?" Before I could respond the guy returned with our drinks. "That is on the house, of course." He informed us. "Will there be anything else?" "If you bring two more beers in about fifteen minutes that will be great. We'll call it quits then." said Tony. The chap gave a very thin smile. "Thank you, sir." He replied and left us to it. "What the hell is going on?" I asked. I truly had no idea what the explanation could be. Tony's smile broadened and gave way to a mischievous chuckle.

"On my way down I needed to go to the loo. I thought I knew where it was, but I opened the wrong door. Instead of entering the toilet I found myself in a small storeroom, but I was not alone. You see the dark haired girl in the black trousers. She is looking this way now." I acknowledged that I knew who he meant. "Well, me laddo was giving her a one to one training session and I accidently eyeballed the whole thing! He seems to be wanting to get on the right side of me for some reason." At this we both burst into laughter and the two accomplices looking over at us knew that they now had two people to worry about. They did not need to be concerned. We had had a laugh at their expense and that was enough. To emphasise this point as we left Tony went over to the guy, who frankly looked terrified, and paid for the drinks.

"Blimey! You're in a generous mood with our money, aren't you?" I said as we got outside trying to needle him. "Christ, their wages are piss poor as it is, without having to pay for our beer as well." I looked at Tony. For all his efforts to appear otherwise deep down he was more of a softie than me. "Anyway, he told me he wanted to marry her!"

Friday 9th July 2004

Rada had not been slow to react to Georgi's phone call and at eight thirty she was on the phone telling us that the preliminary contracts were ready and we should meet her at the Address office at ten to read and hopefully sign them. I asked her if she was aware that we had now agreed to buy a third apartment off plan. "Of course. All the preliminary contracts have been prepared; for this apartment too."

We started to get ready to go to Varna and just as we were about to leave the room the hotel telephone rang. The receptionist informed us that a visitor was waiting for us downstairs. We were not expecting anybody and could not understand who would be calling at our hotel. We went down to reception and were met by the barman from the restaurant where we had spent the previous evening. Tony and I differ in so far as he has long conversations with strangers whereas I am more reserved. The previous evening he had spent about thirty minutes chatting to the barman about our Bulgarian venture and I remember the young man listening very attentively, apparently interested in what Tony had to say. Now this morning he had turned estate agent. He had obviously been very busy after we left him, or more likely that morning, because he was carrying a folder with details about a house he had for sale. Obviously we were not interested, but we were both too polite and, it has to be said, too curious to send him on his way.

We sat down and ordered three coffees from reception. Taking this as a sign that we were receptive to his approach the young barman-cum-estate agent went straight into his spiel. He proudly opened his folder which contained at least a dozen Polaroid shots of the same house, inside and out, with flowery descriptions to accompany each photograph. The descriptions were typed on an ancient typewriter and on about page three the ribbon had obviously started to run dry of ink and handwritten descriptions took over. On several of the pictures an old lady stood smiling for the camera. "Who is the sweet old dear on the pictures?" Tony asked. The young man admitted reluctantly that it was his grandmother. "And does she live there?" I asked, knowing the answer. "And does she know her house is now for sale?" Tony added. "She does not know at the moment, but this is not a problem. She is very old. I will sort this out. Her sister could take her. If you like the house it is yours." "For how much would it be ours?" Tony enquired, his tone starting to show signs of his feelings about this young man and his proposals. "Just twenty five thousand - Euros, of course" "Just twenty five thousand Euros?" Tony confirmed. "Just tell your Granny her house is safe! Come on, Geoff. We have some serious business to see to."

Given we were flying back on Tuesday and the weekend was looming this was effectively our last working day. We told Rada and Georgi this and they made sure that the day was fully utilised. By the end of the afternoon we had signed the preliminary contracts for the two large apartments – interesting, but no hitches here; had eventually signed the preliminary contract for the off plan apartment – plenty of hitches here; had opened a company; had purchased white goods for the large apartments that we intended to let out with Address as our agent; had signed an agency leasing agreement and had given Rada power of attorney to complete on the property deals in the event that we could not make it back for this. In typical Rada style this had all been done without a drink and with no break for lunch.

Usually the signing of preliminary contracts took place at the office of the estate agent, but in an unusual display of power the meeting was arranged by the builder of the two large apartments to take place in his office. Apparently ours was not the only property deal involving this builder to be carried out that day. The builder's office was situated in a prefabricated building in the middle of his yard. We entered through the outer door and were greeted by a young woman who appeared to be a receptionist cum secretary who seated us on some dusty rickety chairs that you might expect to find in any builders office the world over. This did not prepare us for what we encountered next. Having checked with her boss that he was ready to receive us she showed us into a huge room with flowery wallpaper that was dominated by an enormous conference table. At the head of the table sat the builder beneath an almost life size painting of himself. Ignoring Georgi and Rada he greeted Tony and me warmly asking us if we would like some coffee. We thanked him and confirmed that a coffee would be much appreciated. Two minutes later the secretary entered with two coffees and water and placed the cups and glasses before us. Obviously our hangers on would have to go without.

The most staggering thing about the whole proceedings was the process of payment. When the formalities had been completed Georgi indicated that now was the time to pay the deposit and I retrieved the cash from my briefcase that Tony and I had nervously carried across Varna. To mine and Tony's astonishment the builder pulled out an electric counting device of the type they use to count large amounts in banks. He placed the notes in the machine which whirred into action and ten seconds later he stood up from his huge chair and, declaring himself satisfied, shook our hands. Now the preliminary contract was truly complete. I was stunned and remained seated, not quite able to come to terms with the fact that I had handed someone thousands of pounds in cash and had not even received a receipt. I turned to Tony. He had already followed suit behind Georgi and Rada and had got up to leave. "What the hell are we going to tell the group?" I asked still in a state of disarray. "That's an easy one," he replied. "Nothing!"

The most interesting part of the day was the wrangle between Rada and the second builder over the wording of the preliminary contract in respect of the off plan apartment. The preliminary contract is usually simply a description of the property, an agreement by one party to sell and an agreement by the other party to buy. It also usually includes some time frame in which the transfer will be completed, for example, within two months. It is also at this stage that the buyer pays a ten percent deposit which is forfeited if they fail to complete. There is nothing really contentious in this and on Rada's advice we had earlier put our names to the two documents in respect of the finished apartments. When it came to the off plan apartment though things were different.

The first dispute came when Rada refused on our behalf to pay anything up front. The builder was livid and Georgi was certainly surprised. He attempted to act as peacemaker. "Rada, as you know all preliminary contracts are accompanied by a ten percent deposit." He ventured. "Usually, yes." She replied, "But on this occasion what exactly are my clients paying for? He hasn't even started digging the footings!" "Goodwill?" suggested Georgi. "OK. In which case we want a deposit as a sign of the builders good intentions." At this the builder started to lose his temper, but realised quickly that he was wasting his time. This very young innocent looking woman was not going to be the pushover he had expected. Eventually she agreed to a much reduced deposit on the acknowledgement that he had incurred considerable costs at the planning stage. This was only Round one.

Round two was the dispute over staged payments and this argument was considerably more heated than the first. The builder had asked for staged payments at certain intervals of time and Tony and I had already decided off our own bat that we were not agreeing to this. As Rada pointed out: what if by the end of the year he had hardly done anything; should we still pay him? Eventually he agreed to payments being made as the building work reached a particular stage, but what enraged him was Rada's insistence that his outgoings would always outstrip what we were paying him. In other words we should never be making payments ahead of the work completed. When he finally had to swallow this he said he would inform Address when each stage had been completed and they could authorise the next payment. I knew what was coming next: "No, I would prefer it if Address can inform me and, if I am satisfied, I will indicate to my clients that a payment should be made." The builder now reverted to shouting, but it was to no avail. The changes Rada wanted were duly written in and Tony and I obediently signed the contract.

When we said goodbye to Rada Tony, not for the first time, gave her a kiss and as before she looked both embarrassed and quizzical. Reading her expression Tony told her in that convincing way he has that this was a Welsh tradition when taking leave of your solicitor, especially after a deal has been struck. Rada appeared to take this on board and seemed to find it quite quaint. As we left the building I looked at Tony and his silly smile indicated he had anticipated my question. "Since when has kissing your solicitor been a Welsh tradition?" I asked. "It's a well-known fact." He insisted. "I bet you're sorry you are English!" "God, Tony, you're such a charlatan. You are planning to come here with Kay next year. Are you going to kiss Rada then?" This seemed to me a reasonable question. "Of course" he said. "I don't want to disappoint Rada." "So what will you tell Kay" I asked. "That's easy!" he replied. "I'll tell her it's a Bulgarian tradition.

2014: More Traumas; Sweet Arrival

Saturday 5th April 2014: Baile Herculane, Romania to Todorcheta, Bulgaria

At three thirty I was wide awake. Somehow I managed to clear a path to the cooker and to find tea bags and milk. I can put up with almost any level of deprivation, but I *cannot* do without a morning cuppa. So at quarter to four I entered Dracula's lair and found Marieluise's room. I went in to find her sitting on the bed fully dressed and ready to go. She looked on the tea as a small miracle. So we sat there for ten minutes drinking our tea with our own private thoughts, neither of us wanting to talk about the events of the previous night. Knowing Marieluise as a do I realised that her private thoughts about the whole shambles were probably too painful to share and I knew then it would be some time before she would be able to speak about it. That is her way and over the years I have come to both accept that and as far as I can to respect it.

The sheer effort of clearing enough space to have a proper breakfast was beyond us so we fed and watered our beloved creatures and as the first sign of the day appeared in the East we were underway again, still needing to transverse a large stretch of Romania whilst not feeling particularly well disposed towards the country. After about two hours the pangs of hunger started to tell us that we needed a food break. So I pulled in and, as always, the first thing we did was to check the welfare of the horses, although now with more anxiety than erstwhile. As usual they wanted water but were otherwise content. So for the first time in almost twenty four hours we thought about rustling up some food for ourselves.

I now realised that I had undergone a significant change in my whole attitude to the journey. Before we set off I was the one who had done most of the route planning including finding, and booking the overnight stays. Up until our unfortunate Romanian adventure I had been firmly wedded to the plans we had made and to taking appropriate breaks throughout the day. By following this plan we had made good and relatively stress free progress through seven countries, usually arriving late afternoon and finding ourselves able to enjoy the hospitality laid out before us. Now all I wanted to do was keep going. I passed up the opportunity to have a coffee or cup of tea in favour of water that was easier and nearly choked myself trying to get a cheese roll down my neck in less than sixty seconds. With Marieluise only one bite into her roll and the crisp packet as yet unopened I was back in the driver's seat and away.

It is to me a real shame that all these things went wrong in Romania rather than elsewhere. Before we left everyone had warned us about Romania. Don't stop unless you have to; don't trust anyone; don't carry much cash etc. etc. I would have loved for them all to have been wrong and it would have given me great pleasure to report a trouble free trip. The reason I say this is that I am sure a great deal of it is simple prejudice, although those that gave the advice did so in good faith. Once I had cleared my mind a bit from the events of yesterday I started to develop a different perspective. For sure the strong desire to just get to our place in Bulgaria as soon as possible stayed with me, but as we travelled on through this large rambling country I tried to see things how they really were.

Undoubtedly a lot goes wrong here whatever enterprise you undertake and the general competence of the country is relatively low as is the emotional intelligence of some of its people. But why is this? As I have said, because of the poor condition of the roads progress is slow, but this does give you time to take it all in. If you try to exclude the contribution made by man I would say that Romania is in terms of its natural beauty at least as striking of any of the other countries we passed through. It simply has everything. Unfortunately it was ruled by a mad and greedy dictator for many decades; a man that thought all the assets of this beautiful country were his to do as he pleased with. Against the most wonderful landscapes he authorised the building of hideous architectural monstrosities. He randomly displaced people from their homes and he raped the resources of the country for his own

71

gain and self-aggrandisement. After he was gone Ceausescu left the country scarred and impoverished, without the means to get itself back on its feet and possibly even lacking the will to do it. Everywhere you look you see crumbling reminders of his regime; dilapidated and burnt out structures defacing spectacular natural beauty.

Just after midday we arrived at a point where we had to decide whether to continue our eastbound journey across Romania to the Ruse Bridge or to head south and cross into Bulgaria via the new bridge at Vidin. We had a stable booked at Ruse – a Bulgarian friend of Norma Crowe who is a well-established horsey Brit in Bulgaria. Marieluise was in favour of carrying on to there for the scheduled overnight stay. I wish I had listened to her. I was still in the mood of wanting to get to our final destination as soon as possible and wanted to plump for crossing at Vidin. According to the satnav it was only about sixty miles further to Todorcheta, our destination via Vidin than to Ruse. Based on this information I persuaded Marieluise to "go for it" which we did. Unfortunately the satnav information was complete rubbish and we made the wrong choice – or to be more accurate I did.

We turned south and headed for Vidin, a journey of about sixty miles. Soon we found ourselves on the worst road of the entire trip. Bearing in mind this was the main European highway to a brand new bridge across the Danube into Bulgaria one might have expected a decent road, but in typical, Romanian and Bulgarian style they had invested money in the bridge, but not in the roads to it. This is not because they are stupid, but simply that a lot of infrastructure money now comes through the EU and whereas other countries supplement this from their own funds, quite possibly they cannot always afford to do this. Given this I am often surprised that they are allocated the money in the first place. Still the funding relationship between the EU and some of the newer Eastern European members is a book in itself. Is it possible, as many Bulgarians seem to believe, that there is corruption involved in the allocation of contracts for some of these major works and that sometimes part of the budget goes missing? I do not know the answer. To return to the condition of the road, it put me in mind of the type of temporary track that an invading army might lay just to get their supplies across. Again the result was to bring progress down to a crawling pace and therefore the sixty miles took about two and a half hours.

Suddenly as we came closer to the border the condition of the road changed dramatically and we found ourselves on a brand new dual carriageway. We could see the bridge ahead of us and the border crossing just before it. After quite a long wait it was our turn and we were approached by a young friendly Romanian border guard. He looked at out passports, said hello to Bridget and asked us what we had on board. We told him we had two horses to which he replied "Very nice; have a nice day!" and waved us forward on to the marvellous new bridge. This really was an admirable piece of modern architecture. We crossed into Bulgaria and we anticipated another border crossing with Bulgarian personnel. After several miles of travelling along a brand new motorway we finally relaxed and decided that we had passed into Bulgaria unimpeded.

So we had travelled two thousand miles across nine countries and besides at Dover when we were asked to surrender our horse export licence we had not been required to show any document relating to the three animals we were carrying. On the one hand this was good news as on such a journey a lack of hassle is always to be welcomed. On the other hand I felt in some way cheated. We had done so much research for this trip and gone to great lengths to ensure we had every single document that was required and then been asked for absolutely nothing. As an animal lover I also felt a bit concerned that we could travel so far without having to prove that the horses were deemed fit to travel and without even having to prove that we owned them. Still, on balance the lack of hassle won the day and as we progressed further and the new motorway was, against expectations, still stretching ahead of us an air of optimism filled the air. We were in Bulgaria and heading for our final destination with a fair wind.

The motorway continued for about thirty kilometres which was further than I had expected and we then found ourselves on a tolerable single carriageway road. We stopped to feed and water the horses and it was then that we again consulted the satnav. It was still light, but was now late afternoon/early evening and we were not prepared for the news that we had the best part of two hundred miles still to travel. The satnav had been an incredible help all the way along and it did give a warning in Romania and Bulgaria that some parts were not properly mapped and may not be reliable. Our very close Bulgarian friends, Nicky and Dima were already on the way to the house to form a welcoming party, but I don't think they planned to still be there at midnight. Still the dice were cast; we had spurned the opportunity to stop at Ruse and must now plough on.

Suddenly the road came to an abrupt halt with a barrier across it and a dirty hand written sign sending us down a sand track as a diversion. Within one hundred metres we were faced with a fork in the track. I was about to choose what I thought was the most likely option when an old crone strode to the middle of the road indicating the other direction. It looked like the entrance to a quarry, but she was insistent so I followed her instructions. Anyway the only alternative was to run her over and that seemed a bit unfair given she was only trying to be helpful. Another four hundred metres along the track we were faced with a rickety bridge with a sign indicating the bridge was not safe for any vehicle over 3.5 tonnes. I stopped to ponder this dilemma – the only way forward was to ignore the sign, the alternative was to park up and wait the two years that road repairs normally take in Bulgaria. As I sat there worrying I looked up and noticed the vehicle ahead that had crossed the bridge just before me. It was a massive articulated lorry about five times the weight of my vehicle. I crossed.

Not long after this the light began to fade so we stopped for a last time to feed and water the horses. We had a quick bite to eat ourselves and were off again. With still about one hundred and fifty miles to go it was pitch black. Progress was slow enough, but as we got about eighty miles from our goal it started to rain and dense fog descended. Given that we had not had a drop of rain on the whole trip from North Wales to here, this was pretty bad luck. We had no option but to crawl on which we did and at one thirty, in the early hours of Sunday 6th April 2014 our long and eventful journey finally came to an end.

Monday 7th April 2014

From quite early on we had a procession of neighbours calling to welcome us and to introduce themselves. As in the past when we have been here on holiday, the first to see us was our neighbour from the house opposite, known to us as "Honeyman". His actual name is Nicolai. We met him together with his father outside the gate as we were getting something from the car. Honeyman lives most of the week in the nearby town of Gabrovo, but spends as much of his free time as possible in Todorcheta. He grows his vegetables here and has about fifty bee hives. He appears at just about any time, usually accompanied by his father, mother or wife or when things in the garden are busy, all of the above. He can usually be seen wearing a long grey overall in the "Open All Hours" - Ronnie Barker style and a sea captain's cap. He speaks almost no English, but when he meets me he seems to understand enough to take the Mickey and to thoroughly amuse himself. The last time I was here I answered most of his queries with "OK" and so every time he saw me he went, "OK, OK, OK, OK" and then burst out laughing.

On this occasion he lived up to his name by presenting us with a huge jar of honey. I had just five minutes earlier been studying my "Teach Yourself Bulgarian" book and was able to answer with "Blagodarya, e dobre." Which if pronounced properly should convey something like, "Thank you that is nice." This time Honeyman repeated the word "Dobre" over and over whilst laughing like a drain. "Az ucha bŭlgarski" (I am learning Bulgarian) I said trying to regain my dignity. "Dobre, dobre" he again repeated. Then his father interjected with "Mozhe bi mozhete da zapochnete utre" at which point they both lost control and walked away crying with laughter. I did not understand the phrase, but held on to it long enough to get indoors and put it through Google Translate. In answer to my proud assertion that I was learning Bulgarian Honeyman's father had replied, "Maybe you can start tomorrow!"

Within ten minutes, I heard "allo" coming from the gate and a gentleman who I had seen from a distance, but never previously met

75

advanced and greeted us. This was a guy from higher up the hill who introduced himself as "Vlado". I told him our names and after that we were all stumped for words and I was about to fall back on the tried and tested "Dobre" which is much used by Bulgarians, but I feared being the butt of Vlado's humour as well as Honeyman's so I said nothing. Vlado then broke the silence with a long welcome speech of which we understood not a word. Still an inane smile and "Yes, yes" seemed to suffice as a reply and he went off happy.

That same afternoon the sun was shining and we decided to go for a walk through the village. We had only got about forty metres down the hill when another close neighbour called out in English, "Hello you have arrived. How are you?" I replied simply that we were well and glad to be here, but Marieluise took the English she had heard as a cue to start up a conversation. Alas, the lady from Varna had already overtaxed her command of English and looked glum from her lack of understanding. Marieluise, grasping the situation just in time enunciated very clearly, "And how are you?" "Very well, thank you." She replied and her equilibrium and pride were at once restored.

We walked on and around the corner heading for the forest walk when we were summoned over by a hearty looking fellow dressed in what looked like chefs' trousers, a white but grubby tee-shirt and shoes that looked like those worn by china dolls in the fifties. He was most friendly, but alas my attention remained firmly fixed on his shoes for a period of time that exceeded politeness or even admiration.

"My name is Gencho." He asserted and then in a move guaranteed to regain my attention, "My wife English – come!"

We followed him obediently through his gate onto the yard, wondering as we went how we had remained ignorant of an English woman living in our very village. We passed immaculate vegetable plots towards a house with strange oddly coloured shutters to an outside seating area, protected from the sun by a faded pink bed sheet draped over chicken wire. Alongside the ramshackle tables and metal benches was an old but functioning fridge and a telly. On a Hollywood Swing sat a middle aged lady in specs held together by string and tape.

At once Gencho introduced us to his wife, Senka. "I speak the Queen's English." she announced in a heavy accent that at once gave a lie to her assertion. She was indeed very much Bulgarian, but could converse quite competently in English for which we were and remain grateful.

It turned out that Senka was a trained vet which is for us quite reassuring, although she is not in practice, but is rather the Director of an animal research laboratory. As vegetarians and confirmed animal lovers we decided not to probe any further. Senka did, however inform us that a friend of hers was a practicing vet in Gabrovo specialising in horses. Marieluise then ventured the name of a vet that we had been told about during our ongoing preparations for our move. A genuine Bulgarian horseman, Alex Tonev had recommended a horse vet from Gabrovo named Plamen Kolev and indeed this turned out to be Senka's friend. This just added to the dilemma we had over which vet to choose as both Plamen Kolev and a young vet named Momchil had been recommended to us by reliable sources. However, we put that problem aside for another time.

Gencho meantime had a very special surprise up his sleeve. Again we were on our feet following Gencho around to the side of the house where he proudly showed us a beautiful female deer, a young doe standing free not tethered. She was absolutely enchanting and completely unfazed by our presence. Apparently Gencho had found her thin and lost in the forest when very young and took care of her. Now, although she frequently leaves his garden, she always returns. Marieluise was charmed by her, but we left her alone although Gencho assured us that she is quite at ease with humans.

Returning to the outside seating area, Senka had made coffee and was intent on making us very welcome in her village. Gencho and Senka are one of the few couples who live in Todorcheta the whole year round. Gencho looks after the crops in the garden and, like Honeyman, keeps bees, although on a smaller scale, whilst Senka is the breadwinner attending her lab each day. They seemed remarkably content and at ease and we were quite reluctant to leave. When we eventually did, Senka sprung up. "Gencho has a welcome present for you." she exclaimed. She went into the house and emerged with our second jar of honey of the day. What I found really lovely was the fact that she handed it to Gencho to give to us which he did with great ceremony. He keeps the bees and so it was his present. The big question is whose honey will taste best and has the right person been anointed "Honeyman".

So that was a quick round up of our near neighbours, but the head count was not quite complete. After leaving Senka and Gencho's garden we continued our walk a short distance into the forest and then headed back. On returning to the house we realised that our nearest neighbours whose garden overlooks ours were now at home. Plamen and Antonia, who we already know quite well, live in Gabrovo where Antonia is a GP, but take every opportunity to come to the family house, spending on average about ten days per month there. They are, like most Bulgarians, excellent gardeners and as on many previous occasions they presented us with a selection of their produce. Antonia speaks passable German so we can exchange cordial greetings with them and therefore we thanked them for the vegetables without fear of them playfully ridiculing our attempts at their language as Honeyman had done. However, Plamen in his way has made it clear that if we are going to live here he expects to hear Bulgarian spoken.

We went inside, made some toast and pulled out the two jars of honey. After a tasting that we both took very seriously we came to the following conclusion: Gencho is a very able amateur, but Honeyman's title is rightly conferred.

Tuesday 8th April 2014

Waking up today at about half seven I realised why we had made such a monumental trip. There is not a cloud in the sky which is a colour blue that we never or rarely encounter at home. The fruit trees in the yard are in full blossom. Our neighbour, Honeyman, keeps bees and they have temporarily taken up residence in our trees. There is a concerto of humming and the smell from the blossom is divine. Our little Jack Russell, Bridget, has found a spot in the sun, unaware that in a few weeks' time – or even a few days – she will be seeking the shade. The horses are in the paddock adjoining the house and every so often they put their heads over the gate leading to the yard to see what is going on. Already Marieluise is talking about needing to get them in during the day. Does it sound idyllic? Well at the moment it feels that way.

The village of Todorcheta where we are living would hardly qualify as a village back in the UK; it is more just a clump of houses. There is no shop, church or pub and as far as I can ascertain there never has been. There is however a grave yard and as testament to the fact that the same families have lived here for generations most of the graves, including some very old ones are well tended. On a Sunday morning you will always see people working there, tending flowers, cutting the grass and so on. Almost all of the houses in the village were built during the Bulgarian National Revival period, sometimes referred to as the Bulgarian Renaissance. This was a period of considerable socio-economic development and national integration among Bulgarian people under Ottoman rule. It is commonly accepted to have started in 1762 when a Bulgarian monk, Paisius, wrote a landmark book on Slavonic-Bulgarian history and lasted until the Liberation of Bulgaria in 1878 as a result of the Russo-Turkish War. The period is remarkable for its characteristic architecture. The houses usually have two floors and a basement. The first floor is made mainly of stone and has a few small windows, usually barred, as the Bulgarians of the time wanted to protect themselves from their contemporary enemy, the Turks. Some Bulgarians also used the first floor for domestic animals. The second floor is more elegant with large windows divided into small panes. The upper floor projects over the street supported by curved wooden beams. Another typical feature is the roof made from huge slabs of local stone laid across each other with a large stone chimney. Most of the houses have yards surrounded by thick stone walls and entered via large wooden decorated gates.

Our house is from this era and has all the characteristics of a renaissance house. It is one of the grander houses in the village, originally with four bedrooms as well as a "guest house" which is a separate one room building across the yard. This building also houses a huge bread oven. This guest house would have been offered as accommodation to travellers who usually paid for their bed and board by a day's work or by an evening of storytelling to which neighbours might also be invited. We might try this arrangement out when we receive our first visitors from home.

The Guest House

The village is incredibly quiet and many of its inhabitants live in a similar manner to their ancestors. Only about half the village has electricity. Most of our neighbours use lamps and candles in winter, but in summer all of them, including those with a power supply, simply rise and go to bed with the sun. For heating they use entirely wood – in plentiful supply in Bulgaria – which is used to fire at least one stove (pechka) which is also used for cooking. About a year ago Honeyman was connected for electricity and the whole village turned out to witness this monumental step. Since then I have only once seen a light on in his house. The last time we were here we had an unexplained power cut and after about two hours I decided to find out if everyone was affected, not just our house. I went across to ask Honeyman if his electricity was on and he did not know. So far that day he had not had cause to use electricity.

Most houses have no running water; in fact we and one other house have our own well. Everyone else either uses the communal well at the bottom of the village or collects rain water from the gutters of their house and outbuildings into vast water containers of all shapes and sizes. Our immediate neighbours, Plamen and Antonia are the most inventive collectors and users of rainwater I have ever encountered. They have water butts everywhere and even in the driest part of the summer never have less than a thousand litres of water available. Nothing is wasted. For example, they have an outside sink fed from a barrel and as they use the sink the water runs down the plug into a pipe with numerous holes in it that irrigates the vegetable garden. Their prize installation is the outside shower. Their garden, being on the side of a steep hill, is terraced. On the lowest level of the garden a huge flat stone forms the shower platform on which to stand against a six foot high wall that supports the next level of the garden. On this higher level exposed to the sun is a forty gallon plastic barrel which collects water from the roof of their barn. At the foot of the barrel is a tap connected to a long shower hose. The water in the barrel is heated by the sun and with a turn of the tap provides an excellent shower after a long day in the garden. The installation is finished off with a proper shower head holder fitted to the wall and a hook for the towel. There is only one drawback to this near perfect arrangement. Previously our neighbours could shower completely unseen by the rest of the village, but now that we have moved in one has a bird's eye view from our yard. We have tried to alleviate the problem by erecting our gazebo nearby with one closed side forming a partial screen. Despite this Antonia's ablutions have been badly interrupted. Plamen on the other hand gives fair warning by singing or chattering at the top of his voice.

Wednesday 9th April 2014

The track up to our village from the main road is narrow, windy and very steep. It is also pretty knackered. In addition there is not a level bit of ground in the whole of Todorcheta. On the opposite side of the main road the larger village, Rahovtsi, has a large village square. As we approached the village in the early hours of Sunday morning we had already decided that we would park the horsebox there and walk the horses to the house and indeed this is what we did. Later on that Sunday we went down with a barrow and all the normal tools to muck out the box. In the process of doing this some bedding found its way onto the square. Faster than the speed of light a guy appeared and asked in broken English if we were going to clear it up. We assured him we would and he explained that the square was "personal" to him. I took this to mean that he owned or rented it although this seemed unlikely. I have never heard of someone privately owning a village square, but of course this is Bulgaria where different rules apply. He left us soon after, we cleared everything up as we had always intended to do and we thought no more about it, until today.

At about ten in the morning someone came through the gate and called out. It was the village square man. This time he wanted to have a more serious conversation with me and there was no common language to make this possible. Consequently I rang our English speaking Bulgarian friend, Dima, and he earnestly explained everything to her. He handed the phone back to me and as Dima started telling me what he had said, he turned on his heal and left. Outside I heard his car disappearing down the hill. As it turned out he had issued his ultimatum and was not hanging around to negotiate. Dima explained to me without any trace of surprise that he had indeed bought the village square. His plan was to turn it into a paying car park, but the required planning permission had not yet been received. Therefore he could not let anyone park there in the meantime. We had been given two days to move the wagon.

Although the guy thought the whole scheme perfectly plausible, this was to me a typical example of a Bulgarian business project and it both amused and amazed me. As usual no thought had been given to what the market was for this scheme. It had been free to park in the village square for the last twenty years, but except for the odd car stopping to put rubbish into the public bin no one had done so. So on what basis did our earnest businessman think that it would suddenly be a popular parking spot now that he intended to charge for it? The village square has no shop or facility and is five miles from the nearest town. Rahovtsi boasts no more than four or five car owners and they all park outside their house. Perhaps he has heard that Tesco's is opening an out of town store there and it's me that is the idiot. However we now had a more pressing matter to address: where to park our 7.5 tonne horsebox.

Friday 11ᵗʰ April 2014

Today we made a new Bulgarian friend, Vanyo from the village on the other side of the main road. We were just putting the horses into their stables when we heard the now familiar cry of "Allo" from just inside the gate. We looked up to see a tall man in his late sixties approaching confidently. He was dressed just as I remember villagers from Marieluise's home in Germany in the early seventies, i.e. he wore baggy denim trousers, a blue denim jacket and a blue cap. The cap was not in the now familiar baseball style, but had sides and a flat top rather like an upside down shallow saucepan with a peak. Rather incongruously but nevertheless laudable, under the old fashioned denim garb he wore a tee-shirt proclaiming "Peace to the World". He offered his hand and in the manner of one whose appearance had been long anticipated, announced himself as "Vanyo of Rahovtsi".

It soon became apparent that meeting us was not his primary business. Vanyo was a serious horseman and he somehow had prior knowledge of our intention to move here. He had seen the horsebox parked on the businessman's car park that confirmed our arrival. Vanyo was here to meet and greet the horses. "Conete?" he inquired, doing a passable imitation of a horse waggling its ears to ensure understanding. As the compliant hosts that we are we led him to them. On seeing them he went into paroxysms of pleasure. He raised his arms and looked to God in thanks for these heaven-sent creatures. "Bravo, bravo!" he cried and he caressed and stroked them lovingly. Then came the tears of joy. We were genuinely moved by this show of emotion, even devotion to our horses. For their part the horses were so surprised by this unexpectedly lavish attention, they stood stock still and just put up with it. Even when he opened their mouth to undertake a thorough and knowledgeable inspection of their teeth they did not flinch. By a series of gestures and exclamations in his own tongue he thanked us for our indulgence and then he was gone as suddenly as he had arrived. We looked at each other in amazement, but all our feelings about the incident were positive. "Vanyo of Rahovtsi" loved our horses and that was good enough for us.

As we reflected on the visit Marieluise felt she had met or at least seen Vanyo before. We searched our memories and remembered a man who on previous visits we had observed in Rahovtsi herding strangers, including us towards the shop/bar in the hope that they would part with their money at what turned out to be his mother's "Magasin". That man we were sure was "Vanyo of Rahovtsi". From that moment on he was known to us as "Mr Magasin" or just plain "Mr M".

Unfortunately since that time the shop/bar (Magasin) has closed. It closed earlier this year when the old lady who ran it fell ill. There was a small shop with tables, chairs and umbrellas outside. The shop sold all basic provisions and you could also buy beer and wine to take home or to drink on the premises. It was great for an early evening drink and was popular in summer. I was mortified to learn that it had closed. I remember the first time that I approached the shop at about six on an autumn evening. It was already dark and as there were no customers outside and no light was on I assumed the shop was already closed. I was about to turn away when the light suddenly came on. The old lady was sitting in the dark to save electricity and only switched the lights on as a customer approached. I think she must have used the same policy with regard to the fridge, because as I entered the shop the fridge was humming away and the refrigerated beer I bought was at room temperature.

2004: Back Again!
Monday 20th September 2004

For the third time this year we were back for a short visit to Varna to complete the purchases of the two apartments. The builder had allowed Georgi access to the apartments in the period leading up to completion and he was able to tell us that he had carried out our request to have the cookers, fridges and washing machines delivered and installed. We had always known we could trust Georgi, but on this occasion he excelled himself. On our last trip we had gone round with him identifying which cookers, fridges etc. we wanted and noting prices. We had then given him the right money to make the purchases for us. When we met up with him this time we were handed all the receipts which we hadn't asked for or expected and he also returned forty leva, because when he bought the two fridges they were offering twenty leva discounts. He had also ensured that the receipts were proper invoices made out to our company so that we could use them for Bulgarian tax purposes. Even Rada was impressed with this.

After sorting this out Georgi introduced us to a colleague, Ivalyo, who was the firm's letting agent. Georgi said he was a good guy and very good at his job. "He will find tenants for you, for sure." We spoke to Ivo as he was known for some time going through all the details of the contract we had signed last time. He did this very professionally and at the end revealed that he had already identified prospective tenants for each apartment at our asking price of four hundred Euros per month. It was hard not to be impressed with this and as it turned out both of these prospective tenants had signed up by the time we left to go back to Wales.

On the face of it, great, but for some indefinable reason neither of us were sure about Ivo from the start and in all the dealings we subsequently had with him that first impression never left us although we never had anything concrete to base it on. We were made even more uncomfortable when we were required to give him power of attorney to sign tenancy agreements on our behalf. We could see the sense in this as we were thousands of miles away most of the time and both Georgi and Rada said this was normal for overseas clients. We agreed to it, but never liked it. However, we reassured ourselves by remembering that our main business was buying and selling and the rentals were only a side line to help pay our expenses. Nevertheless we now had someone on the "team" that we did not feel comfortable with and this went counter to our carefully laid plans.

Tuesday 21st September 2004

The completion of the purchase of the two large apartments was set for our second day in Varna. Unlike in Britain where completion takes place behind the scenes and involves only the two solicitors, in Bulgaria an almost ceremonious meeting takes place involving the two parties and their respective solicitors, the estate agent and, for deals involving overseas buyers, a state registered translator. The whole thing is presided over by the Notary.

We had already got used to the presence of a translator, because the visits to the notary to arrange powers of attorney also required their attendance. It is hard to argue with this requirement as one could be signing something with no clue as to its contents, but the reality of it for us was extremely tiresome. Rada always gave us a summary of what was going on and we could rely on her to say whether it was safe to sign or not. However, despite this the official translator was required to sit with us and translate the whole document word for word and then sign to say she had done this and we had understood. This had not been too arduous for the powers of attorney, but here we were sitting in front of two five page documents. Our hearts sank as she proceeded. On this occasion there was an added irony in that the official translator's English was much inferior to Rada's and she continually looked up to Rada, who was hovering just behind us, for help. Rada is not the most patient person in these situations and soon she was jumping in every time the translator hesitated even for a moment and then proceeded to finish the paragraph. I am not sure how the translator, a young girl fresh out of college, took these interventions. I think she had mixed emotions, suffering a slight loss of dignity, but also feeling relieved that we were getting through it. Tony and I were just glad that with Rada's help it ended sooner than it otherwise would have.

That night we renewed some old acquaintances at the Fox in Varna. As we entered the place we were given a heroes' welcome, mainly by the landlord whose profit projections for the month went up startlingly as we walked in. As we sat down his eyes darted towards the fridge and he saw with relief that he could at least satisfy our initial order. Without being asked he brought two Zagorkas and two glasses to our table. We were immediately joined by the interpreter and through him we were able to give the landlord the bad news that we were flying home in two nights. This must have spurred him into action. Realising he only had two nights of selling Zagorka he decided the opportunity must be grasped. Immediately the interpreter's nephew was despatched and about thirty minutes later he returned with two crates of the amber nectar and began filling the fridge. Some locals made a fuss as their favourite tipple was removed from the fridge, but the landlord brushed their protests aside with a dismissive wave of the arm.

Minutes later the cook was upon us with a toothless grin clasping her incomprehensible menu. She also was brushed aside. The landlord knew that we would be eating there tonight, but why slow down willing drinkers with the burden of food. The best policy he knew was to allow us to drink enough beer to build up a voracious appetite and deliver the food then. That way we would drink more and eat more. We were happy to oblige on both counts.

Having played a crucial role in furnishing the beer the interpreter's nephew, who was about twenty five, joined us. He spoke quite good English and I must say I was glad of a rest from translating Tony's stories into German because I had either heard them before or I had lived them with him. I also found talking to the young man quite exhilarating as the perspective of young people on their country and its future is of great interest to me. The young man was known as Tosho and he had a lot to say about Bulgaria's recent past as well as its future. He was very politically driven which I found all the more interesting.

His view was that very little would change until the current generation who controlled politics at the local, regional and national level stepped aside or died out as they had all been brought up in a centrally planned economy and could never move fast enough to grasp the new opportunities. He also believed that they were by nature self-seeking and if there were any benefits from becoming westernised the people would never see any of it. Although he was speaking in English his uncle was trying to listen in and occasionally asked him to clarify something he had said in Bulgarian. The young man indulged his uncle's wishes with good grace and I thought the interpreter was also enjoying listening to his nephew. A little later when the young man was chatting to Tony I told the interpreter that his nephew had a lot to say and that I found his ideas very interesting. "You and his father must be very proud of him. He's a good lad." His reply in German was most emphatic: "Er ist *ganz* faul." – He is *completely* idle. He then further clarified his views with regard to his affable young nephew by informing me that modern Bulgaria needed strong men of action not windbags. I think Tosho was correct in at least one thing: there was not likely to be much meeting of minds between the generations regarding the best way forward for their country.

At about half past ten Tony and I were exhausted from our business encounters as well as from our very sociable evening. We decided to make our way back to the hotel, said our goodbyes with a promise that we intended to keep, to be back tomorrow. When we were about half way home we noticed song and laughter coming from just across the square. It was not a bar that we knew, but it seemed lively and we both like live music in almost any form. We decided on one for the road, crossed the square and entered.

It did not take us long to realise that we were not in a bar, but at a private venue. A man on a keyboard and a female vocalist were playing some old Beatles songs in the form of a medley and the guests seemed to be enjoying it. A few were dancing. Nevertheless, realising our mistake we turned to leave. "Good evening!" The greeting came from across the hall and many of the guests turned to look at us. I was not for the first time left wondering what it was that made us so easy to recognise as British. "Where are you from?" called the young woman with a welcoming smile. "We are from North Wales." replied Tony with that slight puffing out of the chest that always accompanied an expression of his nationality. "Yes, I know Wales. I once stayed in Cardiff. And where are you going?" "We did not realise it was a private party" I said. "I am sorry. We are just leaving." "Why are you leaving? It is my sister's wedding. She loves the British. Stay!" Then in an aside almost to herself, she asked "Where is Katrina anyway?" A younger woman strongly resembling the first speaker gave a languid wave from the dance floor. "Stay and have drink. I love you." Well what could we say? That was definitely the best invitation to a party either of us had ever received.

2005: New Discoveries; Dodgy Tummies

Monday 23ʳᵈ May 2005

This summer Tony and I had agreed that I would make an early trip to Bulgaria without him combining a business trip with a holiday with my wife, Marieluise. The plan was that Tony and Kay would do likewise in 2006. However both our wives had been warned that we always had quite a bit of stuff to sort out and given everything in Bulgaria took so long to complete it might end up more business than pleasure. Nevertheless, both Marieluise and Tony's wife Kay were keen to see this place that their husbands now talked about incessantly. It was my turn first and Marieluise and I duly arrived in Varna. Like Tony and I last time we had booked a package holiday in a resort near Varna, this time it was Albena. As we were coming in to land Marieluise was amazed to see so many high rise flats. On one level she was of course aware of the tendency of Eastern European states to house their people in this way, but the scale of it and the predominance of these types of buildings away from the city centre can take you by surprise. In fact I had become so used to moving around in the centre I had myself become immune to this phenomenon and landing in Varna for only the second time I was somewhat taken aback by it too. We landed and soon found ourselves on the transfer bus heading for Albena.

Albena was an upmarket version of Golden Sands with less tat and more open spaces. Our first impression of the place was quite pleasing. We were tired from an early start and long flight, but equally we were keen to have a look round. After a shower and change of clothes we headed into the resort and immediately struck gold. As we approached a fairly unassuming bar/restaurant we saw a sign proclaiming "Elvis is in the building!" We immediately took a table and before we had even ordered our first drink an Elvis from the Las Vegas days appeared on stage in a shiny gold jump suit, but rather surprisingly with a blonde wig. Bulgarians never quite get these things right. As an Elvis lookalike he was pretty rubbish and he was dressed for the wrong era given he was singing songs from Elvis' early career, but as a performer he was pretty good. We enjoyed the evening, but I must admit I never quite came to terms with the blond hair. Still for the holiday part of our trip it was a pretty good start. It pleased me too that Marieluise's first impression was positive, but she had already experienced the quirkily flawed way that everything is done in this unique and strangely lovable country.

We had been given a nice hotel and as we had stayed up later than planned we fell into bed and were soon asleep. I woke up several times though conscious of all the tasks that Tony and I had agreed I should complete.

Tuesday 24th May 2005

I had a prearranged meeting with Rada as there were all sorts of things to sort out. There was council tax due on the two large apartments; company declarations to make; company taxes to pay and most importantly the third apartment was now finished and the deal had to be completed. I had also arranged to meet Georgi and Ivo at Address. I wanted to go with Georgi to see the small apartment before agreeing the completion and I wanted to review the balance sheet that Ivo had sent to me regarding income from the rentals. Before seeing him I wanted to go to the bank to check our balance so that I could see that the payments he referred to had gone in. So on day one at least Marieluise was not going to do much in the way of sightseeing. I offered her the option of staying at the resort, but she was keen to meet the people that I was always talking about. To put it in her words she wanted to see if Rada was as pretty, Georgi was as sharp and Ivo was as smooth as I had claimed.

We got up later than planned so after a quick breakfast we were looking for a taxi to Varna. In recognition that we were supposed to be on holiday I had not asked for an alarm call and as a result we had overslept. This was a fatal mistake on my part as Marieluise hates nothing more than rushing, especially in the morning. I was lucky though. A rushed start to the day usually puts her in a bad mood, but once we got outside the warmth and the cloudless sky worked its wonders and the hurried breakfast was forgotten. To save time I desisted from haggling with the taxi driver and paid for this with a fare of thirty leva. I made a mental note not to let this happen again. I would have to avoid this particular taxi driver on subsequent mornings as I had now handed him the advantage and reduced my bargaining power.

It was really lovely to see Rada again and she welcomed Marieluise equally warmly. They got on really well, but Rada is very business-like and soon we were going through our mutual agenda. Most importantly she told me that completion had been set for tomorrow, but agreed that I should first of all see the apartment for myself. She also told me that the builder needed part of the balance that we still owed in cash so the ritual of previous deals was about to be played out again. We agreed to meet the following day at her office and Marieluise and I left to go to the Address agency via the bank.

At the bank I learned that the correct payments had been made by Ivo albeit in one lump sum just before we arrived. I was already a little surprised with the level of deductions he had made and this discovery of the one very late payment put me further on my guard. I did not draw out the Euros in cash that I needed for the deal on the following day because I hate carrying so much money around for so long. Instead I decided that I had time for this before meeting Rada in the morning.

When I arrived at the Address office I asked to see Georgi, but Ivo appeared first wearing a beaming smile. I introduced Marieluise and he greeted her as if he were meeting the Queen. Once we got down to business he had a ready answer for everything I asked him and in the end I just decided I couldn't be bothered arguing with him. The fact was we were only using the money to pay the day to day business expenses and given how low these costs were in Bulgaria what we were earning from the flats was more than adequate to cover everything. To avoid hassle I just let it go.

Soon Georgi joined us and we departed to look at the apartment. The builder had done a great job and I was now more than happy to go ahead with completion. Also I could see that it would be easy to let the flat out so a little extra for us and of course another deal for Ivo.

Wednesday 25ᵗʰ May 2005

Not making the same mistake as yesterday we were up early and had a leisurely breakfast before heading for the taxi rank. My heart sank when I saw that only one taxi was waiting and it was the same driver as yesterday. This made negotiations very difficult, but there was no way I was going to pay thirty leva every day. In the end I had to walk away in order to get it down to twenty. This still seemed a lot, but Albena was quite a way from Varna so I settled on it making it clear that I was only paying this amount on each subsequent trip. At first in Bulgaria you see the taxi negotiations as an enjoyable challenge, but to be honest it was starting to get me down. Taxi fares are supposedly regulated, but in reality the regulations are never enforced so this tiresome process is re-enacted every time you travel. It is just one more thing that needs to be sorted if Bulgaria is serious about becoming a tourist destination.

Our first call was to the bank and immediately the drama began. Given that we had made staged payments already only the final balance was due. No they could not transfer any of the money into the builder's account and no they could not give me the balance in cash from my own account. I should have given them forty eight hours' notice. I started to argue, but could see it would be hopeless. Reinforcements were required in the form of Rada. We left the bank and arrived early at her office. Rada was neither surprised nor fazed by this information. She simply picked up her papers, put on her jacket and accompanied us back to the bank. She made the same request and was met with the same answer. Everything that followed took place in Bulgarian so I can only report on the number of people involved, tone of voice and so on. In summary, four members of the bank staff were involved, everyone shouted at everyone at the end of which Rada told me where to sign and a letter was handed over confirming a transfer of funds to the builder's account, incidentally a customer of the same bank. The original member of staff was not finished yet and as we left she shouted something to us which did not even cause Rada to look round. Marieluise on the other hand was in a state of shook, but nevertheless triumphant and certainly very impressed with our Rada.

After all the excitement at the bank the actual completion went off without a hitch. The letter confirming a transfer of funds was handed to the builder and I saw him smile for the first time since I had met him. He shook my hand and left the Notary's office studying the bank transfer document for the third time as he went. I handed the keys to Georgi and asked him to enlist Ivo to try and get a tenant. I did not have the energy or the inclination to see Ivo again. I think Georgi understood this and with a soft knowing smile he nodded his agreement.

So after a difficult day Marieluise and I decided we would head back to the resort and give ourselves a proper evening out. The last time we had done this we had immediately bumped into Elvis so we left the hotel with hopes high. Again we were not disappointed. About ten minutes' walk from the hotel we came across a large bar with a stage and some Latin music in full swing. As we entered we saw about ten youngsters on stage dancing the Cha-cha and they were very good indeed. Marieluise and I are Ballroom and Latin dancers and so there could not have been a better form of entertainment. Soon we realised that it was better than we had imagined because about ten minutes later they invited members of the audience onto the stage and we were able to get up and strut our stuff. After about fifteen minutes the music stopped and we went to our table to order some food and lo and behold the dancers who had been on the stage were now waiters and those who had been waiting at the tables became dancers. All the youngsters had their names on their backs and soon we were able to pick out the really exceptional ones, although they were all very talented. It was an amazing idea and they were three times busier than any rival restaurant. We had a brilliant evening and something to tell our dancing friends back at home.

Thursday 26th May 2005

By nine thirty we were in Varna at the same small agency where Tony and I had hired a car last year. Confirming my belief that they were hiring out their own private car we were again allocated the only car on the forecourt. This time we were hiring it for two days so it would be the bus home tonight for the two young women running the agency.

Tony and I had spoken already about exploring possibilities in the historic town of Veliko Tarnovo and I had been entrusted with the first look. It was about a two hour drive from Varna so we set off as soon as the formalities of the car hire had been completed. We were about one hour into the journey when the engine started missing. I looked down at the dashboard to check for warning lights, but there was no indication of a fault. What I did notice, however, was that the "hire car" had over three hundred thousand kilometres on the clock. I stopped and looked up the telephone number that I had been given for emergencies. A young man answered and thankfully he spoke quite good English. I explained the problem and he did not really know what I was rabbiting on about. He understood what I was saying, but he was nothing to do with any hire firm and was not a mechanic. As we spoke further the penny dropped for both of us and it turned out he was the boyfriend of Lyudmila, the younger of the two agency girls. He said he knew a bit about cars and would be happy to come out, but given that firstly, we would be waiting forever, secondly he probably knew no more than me and thirdly the car was still going, we decided to press on. Marieluise felt we had been swindled, but I having had more exposure to Bulgaria found the whole thing hilarious. We started the car and coughed and spluttered our way to Veliko Tarnovo.

What a place! With the houses draped across the cliffs above the river Yantra, it was magnificent.

The beautiful city of Veliko Tarnovo

They say that first impressions are important and that first day I saw Veliko Tarnovo I fell in love with it and still regard the town as having a unique charm and beauty. Parts of it are crumbling away, but this adds to rather than detracts from its charm. Veliko Tarnovo was the capital of the Second Bulgarian Empire and has long traditions in the culture of Bulgaria. The city is rich in historical sites. "VT" also boasts one of the largest universities in Bulgaria. The old city is where the charm lies and consists of a collection of traditional renaissance houses scattered over the hills around the river Yantra. The jewel in the crown is Gurko Street, named after the Russian, General Gurko who "liberated" the Bulgarian people in 1878 defeating the Turkish occupiers. The street is narrow and roughly cobbled and struggles to accommodate the cars that attempt to drive along it. In fact the best way to see the old town is on foot and this is what Marieluise and I set out to do. Given the layout of the city, built on the hills around the river, moving from street to street involves climbing up and down and one passes from one level to another via ancient sets of steps that wind their way through the small houses. To say we were enchanted by the place would be an understatement.

However, I had to remind myself that I was here to review the property market not as a tourist and we had very little time to hang out in the small bars and cafes that were dotted everywhere around the town. That could come later. With an admirable resolve I told a reluctant Marieluise that it was time to look for the Address estate agency. Georgi had proudly informed me that they had expanded considerably since I first encountered them and that included into VT. It did not require a great effort on our part to find it. We walked into the town's central square and the large blue letters proclaiming "Address" were plain to see.

We went into Address to enquire about properties, but once we introduced ourselves it was not necessary to say in any detail what we were looking for. Georgi had been in touch and they were ready for us with an agent set aside and a list of properties to view. As the young agent, the beautiful Kremena, did not have a licence a driver had been laid on too. There was no mention of agency contracts or deposits. They were ready to roll. They had agreed with Georgi to show us village properties around VT today and then properties in the old town tomorrow. I would have preferred it the other way round, but rather than be churlish I agreed that their plan was perfect. Within minutes we were in the back of a sign written people carrier heading out of the city.

Kremena was chatting away, apparently quite excited to have us there which if Georgi had told her anything about our buying history was hardly surprising. She told us where we were heading, but it meant nothing to me and even today I find it hard to retain the names of villages until I have heard them a few times. So I cannot recall the name of the first village we entered, but I can vividly recall the house. When we arrived it seemed as if the whole extended family were there to meet us. There were at least twelve of them. They took us in through the front door, before I had a chance to even look at the outside and proceeded to move from room to room as a hoard with Marieluise and I sort of locked between them. The thing that most struck me, although not relevant to my property quest, was the absolute paucity of the furniture. In the corner of the main room was an ancient blackened stove (a pechka) and close to was an old table which on closer inspection turned out to be an old piece of board on top of two metal barrels. The seating around the table consisted of a motley selection of anything that had a flat top and would stand upright; upturned beer crates and orange boxes with planks across them were favourite. Entering the bedrooms we saw a variety of cots, couches and paillasses and in one room just heaps of blankets on the ground. In place of wardrobes and chests of drawers were rusty upright tool drawers and a variety of plastic, wooden and metal boxes. Rather incongruously a "My Little Pony" stable and horses sat immaculate amongst the assorted rubble. Of bathrooms and toilet there was no mention.

Eventually I broke free from my captors and was able to tell Kremena that I wanted most of all to look at the outside. I was aware that if we purchased a village house it would most certainly need a full programme of renovation as this house viewing confirmed. I was therefore more interested to see the outside to firstly check it was structurally sound and secondly to ascertain if it had something in terms of character and style to recommend it. Kremena, Marieluise and I went out followed by the family and after a brief perusal we could see that it was a fairly plain house, square and stout. We went around the back and this told a different story. There was an enormous crack in the rear wall from top to bottom. It was so bad that the two sides of the crack were falling into each other and the roof was six inches lower on one side. From the inside the crack had been hidden by the staircase the underside of which I could now see through the crack. Although I was reasonably brave when it came to looking over old or even derelict houses I felt a cold shiver when I realised that ten minutes earlier we had been ascending the stairs without a care. We could have been the last people ever to do so. Seeing my look of alarm one of the younger men in the family stepped forward to reassure me. "No problem. When you buy wall fixed." Somehow I did not think it would be that easy.

As we were leaving the same young man asked me if we were buying it. The whole group seemed to think that I would slap some notes in their hand there and then and waited expectantly for my answer. I was about to say, "You must be joking!" or words to that effect when Marieluise intervened. "We will discuss it with Kremena and she will let you know." She had sensibly realised that if I said "No" we could be there all day arguing about it. I left it at that and before the matter went any further Kremena bundled us into the car, spoke some rapid Bulgarian to our hosts and we were away.

"So how much did they think they would get for that?" I asked not hiding my irritation. "Twenty thousand Euros. What did you think?" I was frankly surprised to hear Kremena ask this, in fact I was quite annoyed by the question. "What I think is this: You either revise your plans for the day and show us some reasonable properties at Bulgarian prices or you take us back to VT now." Marieluise was equally clear. "Look Kremena, Geoff has been looking at Bulgarian property for a year now and before that for a long time on the net. We know you can get some nice older properties for less than half that price so stop messing us about." Kremena mumbled a half apology saying she did not realise the house was so bad and then gave an instruction to the driver that caused him to stop and turn round. There had obviously been a change in plan.

From then on things changed and we were shown some lovely rural properties at reasonable prices, some of them built during the Bulgarian National revival, also known as the Renaissance period, with the distinctive architectural features of the period. All of them needed considerable renovation work, but they were all structurally sound. I said no more to Kremena about the first house she showed us as I was confident there would not be a repeat of such a fiasco. One of two of the houses was particularly attractive, but we gave Kremena very little feedback. We wanted to consider the wisdom or otherwise of investing after we had been shown some town houses which was due to take place the following day.

That evening we walked for miles around Veliko Tarnovo, fascinated by the steps and narrow streets that were such a feature of the city. When we came upon the same small restaurant overlooking the river for the third time we decided it was an omen and went in for a meal. There were only three tables on the lovely little terrace and we were pleased to see one of them free. The view from our table was magnificent giving a panoramic view of a large part of the old town and the river below. Whilst we were waiting for our food to be brought I wandered inside for a look. The walls of the restaurant were actually the rock face giving the impression of being inside a cave and so henceforth we always referred to the place in that way; from that moment on it was known as the "Cave" and to this day I do not know its real name. Earlier that day we had stopped with Kremena for a quick lunch in a small rather grubby looking village bar. I recall that we had the Bulgarian equivalent of a toasted sandwich and from late afternoon we had both been feeling a bit queasy and below par. As a result we had only a couple of drinks at the Cave with a salad and a bowl of chips between us.

Quite early on we returned to our hotel which had been chosen for us by Kremena. She told us that although she had never been inside all the people coming in and out looked very "shiny".

Unfortunately the prices were pretty sparkling too, but it had been too late to find an alternative. By the time we got to our room we cared little about the room or the hotel itself as we were now suffering what we could only assume was full blown food poisoning brought on by our dubious lunch. The room that we became most familiar with during a disturbed night was the bathroom.

Friday 27th May 2005

After a terrible night we both fell into quite a deep sleep at about six in the morning, but alas when we woke up again at eight the symptoms had not left us. I was feeling a little better, but Marieluise was still in a bad way. Kremena would have to wait. The first visit had to be to the chemist and I was nominated as the one most likely to make it there and back without a mishap. The receptionist told me where the nearest chemist was – not too far – and off I went. On the way I kept thinking, "Please let them speak English!" but my luck was out. After trying without success to make myself understood I had no alternative but to resort to mime. It is rare for me to feel embarrassment, but as I went into a full performance I did go a little red in the face although whether it was from embarrassment or exertion I cannot tell. Firstly I mimed someone eating, then I rubbed my stomach and groaned and finally I demonstrated how I had been firing from both ends. Sound effects were also provided. The chemist, a slim well-dressed woman of about forty did her best to withhold a laugh, but in the end it just burst forth like a dam giving way and she could hardly get her words out. When she did I realised the whole pantomime had been completely unnecessary. "Imodium. Tryabva Imodium." I did indeed need Imodium and now realised that I could simply have asked for it by name. Instead I had made a complete ass of myself.

She went and got a packet from the shelf, but my problems were not yet over. I indicated that I wanted two packets and she was trying to explain to me that I only needed one dose. It appeared that as a conscientious chemist she was not willing to give me a higher dose than I needed. I tried several languages to explain there were two people in need. "I need a packet for me and one for my wife." No response. "Für mich und auch für meine Frau." Still she withheld the second packet. "Ma femme!" Nothing. "For me and for my woman." This was my last hope. "Ah, fat woman, OK." Mysteriously she then handed me two packets of Imodium with no further concerns. I had no idea why the non-existent fat woman had been the key, but I was not staying to find out. She asked for sixteen leva, I gave her a twenty and rushed from the shop, booty in hand, without waiting for my change.

I arrived back at the hotel to find Marieluise back in bed holding her stomach and groaning. I held my trophy aloft leaving her to wonder why I regarded two packets of the foul Imodium as such a prize. She snatched a packet from me and headed for the bathroom. The instructions indicated that only one or two tablets were required; she took three. I took the correct dosage and we both returned to bed with hope in our heart. By ten o clock we still felt awful, but the firing from both cylinders had ceased. I phoned Kremena, apologised for our lateness and said we would meet her at about eleven. She seemed relieved; she had probably thought she was not going to see us again.

At just gone eleven we crawled from our room and went down to check out. At eleven fifteen we were sitting in Kremena's office, white faced but otherwise intact. She had a file ready with pictures and details of a number of houses in the old part of Veliko Tarnovo. She was wildly enthusiastic about the day ahead. "I have the driver standing by if we need him. I suggest you pick out five or six properties from what I am going to show you and then we can go and visit them." I started to go through the information laid out before me, but I just wasn't well enough. I put the file aside and looked at Kremena. "I know you have gone to a lot of trouble, but we haven't really got enough time. We need to get the hire car back to Varna tonight." This was not strictly true, but we had decided on this course of action. "Have you any houses in Gurko Street?" Kremena picked up the file and quickly found the only property in that street. "Let's take a look." I suggested.

We unnecessarily got into the car for what turned out to be a journey of less than half a mile. On the way there Kremena explained that there was currently a tenant living in the house, a young single mum with a boy of about seven. I asked whether she knew we were coming as I did not recall Kremena phoning anyone. "She knows the house is for sale." was Kremena's reply. Evidently the tenant was not aware of our imminent arrival and I seemed to be the only one who thought it mattered.

We parked the Address vehicle in the narrow road leaving enough room for a 2CV to pass but not much else. The driver got out too and led the way. From the outside the house looked tiny and unassuming. It appeared to have only one storey, but Kremena had been insistent that it had two. I was intrigued. I was standing there like an idiot, still unhappy about the tenant not knowing we were coming when the driver gave a smart rap on the front door and without waiting for a reply opened it and walked in shouting, "Agentsiya!" by way of introduction. On the whole it seemed a bit late to be introducing oneself. We had no option but to dutifully follow. At once the mystery of the two stories was solved. One entered from the street onto the upper level of the house and then went downstairs to the other storey which had windows facing out to the river.

The young woman was given no explanation as to what we wanted; she was not asked if it was convenient and frankly she looked terrified. Marieluise and I said hello in as cheerful a way as we could under the circumstances and tried to engage with the little boy which was difficult given the language barrier. For his part the young lad seemed disinclined to leave his mother's side. You could hardly blame him. The house was in an appalling state and in my opinion the current owner and landlord should have had a lot to answer for. In all my years in family and child care social work I had never seen a house so completely unsuitable for a mother and young child. There was an old rusted oil tank in the hallway that I assume had at one time been a source of oil for heating. It was leaking slightly and the whole place smelt of oil. I found myself hoping to God that the woman did not smoke. The toilet was mounted on some sort of plinth with no door or even walls separating it from the other rooms. On the lower floor one could look across to the widows that looked onto the river and Marieluise approached the largest window to see what the view was like. The floor slopped acutely towards the window and as she got closer she stopped in horror. The so called window was no more than a square hole in the wall, with no frame or glass. One could easily pitch straight out of the window with a sheer drop to the rocks below.

Amidst all the anxieties about the tenant and her son living here I had somehow to concentrate on the house. This was after all a property viewing. Also I was aware that there would be people living like this all over VT and likewise in other towns across Bulgaria.

The little house had great possibilities and through all the crap and the chaos I was able to imagine how it *could* look. It was for sale for just five thousand pounds so it was hardly a risky purchase in the greater scheme of things. And it was in Gurko Street the most picturesque and historic street in the town. At the back of my mind was also the possibility of doing it up and offering it back to the tenant, but if I made a decision on this basis I would have Tony to answer to.

103

Outside I checked the price with Kremena and when she confirmed it I said I would buy 34 Gurko Street. "Do you not want to see any others?" she asked, but I did not. I was still not feeling well and exposure to any more scenes like I had just witnessed required a stronger stomach than mine in its present state. Kremena then requested that we return to the office to formalise the agreement and pay a holding deposit. This I did not want to do and anyway we were both eager to get going, especially bearing in mind that the car was likely to play up again. "I don't want to appear awkward, but I do not see the need for it. It is sold and I won't be going back on it. I will give you the contact details for my solicitor and you can agree a preliminary contract with her. If you are not sure about all of this just ring Georgi Koev in your Varna office. He will tell you not to worry." With that we wished her a good afternoon and made our exit leaving her to decide whether or not she had made a sale. She had.

Monday 19th September 2005

A lot had happened since my last visit with Marieluise. Rada had used her power of attorney to complete the purchase of the house in Gurko Street. On my instructions Address had offered the tenant the opportunity to stay on, but realising that we were going to undertake some major renovations she had decided to move in with her mother. With that matter cleared up we were now free to consider what work we wanted to undertake on our new acquisition. We had decided to try and get estimates for the renovation of the house and with that in mind and other business to see to we had landed in Sofia today.

From the airport we had secured an OK Supertrans taxi via the little booth in the arrivals lounge and had been taken to the bus station in the city for the correct fare of twelve leva. There we purchased two tickets to Veliko Tarnovo and were told the bus was due in thirty minutes at bus stop number nine. So far so good. We went upstairs for a quick coffee and fifteen minutes later we went outside to wait for our bus. As we approached bus stop number nine we saw what we assumed was our bus sitting at bus stop seven. It was an Etar bus clearly marked up front as travelling to Veliko Tarnovo and then onto Varna. It was no surprise to us that it was at the wrong bus stop. This was Bulgaria. It would have been a bigger surprise to find it waiting in the right place. We were about to board when Tony quite sensibly took our tickets to the driver to check it was correct. Immediately the driver started shouting at the top of his voice pointing furiously to another bus, not parked at any bus stop just against the far kerb. This bus marked Varna was apparently ours. Tony never appreciates being spoken to in this way and just about keeping his temper in check he tapped the guy on the shoulder and insisted he come to the front of his own bus. There Tony pointed with a questioning gesture at the board proclaiming the destination. With no smile, no apology in fact no acknowledgment at all the driver went inside the bus, changed the destination to Plovdiv and walked away to carry on with his business. Being polite and helpful to his customers was evidently not part of that business. Soon we were on the correct bus on our way to VT.

Three hours later we stepped from the bus into the glorious heat and sunshine that we had now come to expect in Bulgaria. It was just after five and there was a very inviting bar just across from the bus station named the Humphrey Bogart. The umbrellas indicated the availability of our favourite tipple, Zagorka. Without actually discussing it we went across and took a table outside. As had become our custom we sat at a table half in and half out of the shade. Tony as always sat in the direct sunlight while I preferred the more sensible option of sitting under the umbrella. This was Tony's first trip to VT and after a pint I thought he would be anxious to have a look round. When I suggested this to him his response was classic Tony. "I'm looking around now. I love it already." With that he ordered two more large Zagorkas.

When we were ready to get going we realised we still needed to find a hotel. I remembered a beautiful authentic Bulgarian hotel somewhere in the old town. I was sure I could find it. Tony was aware of my sense of direction from walking around Varna and other towns for hours on end. He was not prepared to take the chance. There was a very drab multi storey hotel close by. We could see it from where we sat. "That's our hotel for the night and this is our bar for the night. I'll go and book us in. You get the ale in!" "Don't you want to see the house?" I enquired. "Yes, very much – tomorrow." What could I say? Nothing, as far as Tony was concerned the subject was closed.

Tuesday 20th September 2005

The hotel was drab and utilitarian. The breakfast was adequate, but uninspired. After half a dozen Zagorkas the night before, downed in record time it hardly mattered. I had made an appointment with Address for eleven o clock so we had time to kill. We checked out of the hotel, left the bags with the hotel reception and headed into the old town with a view to showing Tony his new house and finding the authentic Balkan hotel that I had wanted to look for last night. Tony had been right not to trust me. I found Gurko Street alright, but after an hour searching I could not identify the house. "The place must have made a lasting impression on you." Tony quipped as I finally gave up and went in search of the hotel. Tony learns fast. He returned to the bar where we had spent the previous evening and ordered a coffee. "Let me know when you find it." he said emphatically and settled down for what he assumed would be a long wait. I was back forty minutes later with no more success than I had enjoyed looking for the house. I tried to defend myself saying I had been both ill and in a hurry when I was last here, but it was too late. He had already stored the story away for telling back at the Fox, our local in North Wales. I could see his little brain working already on the embellishments he would employ as he told the story. I had been a prat so I would just have to take it on the chin.

By the time I had ordered and drunk a coffee it was nearly eleven o clock. I was already sweating that I wouldn't be able to find the Address office, but as we stood to go I looked up and saw it fifty metres away. "I trust you can find the Address office?" Tony enquired without much confidence. "Of course I can. Do you think I'm stupid?" There was no immediate reply then after a long pause he said. "As it happens, it doesn't matter because I know where it is." And as had been our custom when trying to find places in Bulgaria we left the bar with me following him.

Since my last visit there had been changes at Address too. The beautiful Kremena had decided that she knew all there was to know about running an estate agency and had set up on her own as "Classic Bulgaria". I had already received a stream of e-mails from her with pictures of what she hoped would be irresistible properties. However, I had not responded as Tony and I had long ago thrown in our lot with Address and as we were now paying only half the normal commission we were not about to change. I had therefore been in touch with the beautiful Kremena's replacement at Address, a woman known as Desi. From just a few e-mails I could tell that she spoke excellent English and also that she had a sense of humour. I was looking forward to meeting her.

We arrived at the Address office on time and asked for Desi. Thirty seconds later she emerged smiling from the back office. Desi was young and lively. She spoke English as well as I did albeit with a slight American twang. We both liked her instantly. She got three coffees from the machine and we sat down to discuss business. "OK, what can I do for you guys?" "Well, helping us find our new house would be a start! Geoffrey here could not find it, nor the hotel for that matter." Obviously Tony had no intention of sparing my blushes. Desi for her part found this hilarious and made no attempt to hide it. "Yes, that sounds like a good start." she agreed. "And then?" I decided to jump in at this stage before the two of them completely set the tone at my expense. "And then we would like you to recommend a builder who could renovate the house at a good price. As you know it needs a hell of a lot of work." Desi now became very business-like. "OK. We have a builder that we usually recommend. We can go to the house now – it is only a ten minute walk – and I will ask the builder to join us at twelve. This will give you a chance to have a good look round and decide what work you want doing." "Sounds like a plan." said Tony and off we went.

Seeing the house from the outside I could tell that Tony was a little unsure, but he said nothing. When we got inside he realised that the house had a storey below the street that was open to the river. "Ah, I get it now." He said with some relief and as he looked round he too could see the character in the house despite the mess. By the time the builder arrived we had a pretty good idea how we wanted the house to look and Desi was fully in the picture and ready to translate. The builder was an upright man of about fifty who took the instructions from Desi with little comment other than to say that what we wanted was definitely doable. He did however take a lot of notes which we were pleased about. He walked around the house several times, measured up to enable him to calculate the overall size of the building and declared that he had the information he needed to draw up an estimate. On enquiry he surprised us by saying the estimate would be ready in two hours, although of course it will be written in Bulgarian. At this he gave what could almost be described as a smile. It was agreed that he would get the estimate to Desi and we would meet her again at her office just after three.

"So which hotel are you looking for?" Desi asked. "That's part of the problem," replied Tony. "Einstein here can't remember what it is called." "That's not quite true." I objected. "I have never known the name I just saw it somewhere as I was walking around." "It sounds to me as if you need a detective to help you, not an estate agent! What is it like?" Desi was trying to be helpful, but aimed to get all the humour out of this situation that was possible. "It is quite large, built in the Renaissance style and inside it is sort of Balkan looking." I was reasonably confident about my description. Desi smiled to herself. "You may not need a detective after all." she said with a mischievous air. "Let's go!" We walked outside turned left and twenty metres along stood the hotel. "Could this be it?" she enquired, biting her lip to stop herself laughing. I went bright red, Tony fell about and Desi, as if nothing was amiss said, "See you guys at three." To make matters worse I looked up at the hotel and saw the name: "The Gurko Hotel". I had bought a house on Gurko Street and failed to find either the house or the hotel bearing the same name. What a plonker.

At three o clock we were back at Desi's office and to our amazement the estimate was typed out and ready. Desi started to translate it, but Tony stopped her. ""For the time being Desi just tell us how much it comes to, please." "Just under thirty one thousand Euros." Tony and I looked at each other. It was a small house, but this was a complete renovation, inside and out and the price was about twenty two thousand pounds. It would cost three times this at home, maybe more. "How much is materials and how much is labour?" Tony asked, but Desi explained that it was not laid out like that: each individual piece of work was itemised and priced, but it did not divide materials and labour. She then proceeded with a full translation. Itemised it was easier to compare with prices at home and it seemed even cheaper. "We'll give you a ring in a bit." I said. "We need to have a think."

Tony and I went for a beer. It was a little early, but it helps relax you and eases clear thinking. I know that most medical men would refute this theory, but it works for us. Also the price of the pint, around thirty pence, helped us to get the right perspective. I was the first to speak. "The estimate seems very good, but we are not comparing like with like. Think of the price of this beer. It is not 2005 here. We are in the equivalent of the late seventies. What would a British builder have estimated then?" Tony agreed. "And the house was only five thousand quid. It seems a bit out of kilter. Also of course it is likely that the agents are getting a wedge for putting him forward." "No doubt." I replied. "And there is a good chance that his prices are geared almost entirely to the British market. That is where the work is at the moment." We talked and talked and as we did so we became more convinced that we could do better. We needed to talk with Desi again.

I called Desi and said we wanted to take her for a coffee. We walked to her office and as we approached we saw here outside having a cigarette. Like ninety percent of Bulgarians she smokes heavily. We said hello and then I put the following question to her: "If your father was having work done at home, say an extension or a garage, who would he get to do it?" For the first time Desi looked a bit uncertain. "Maybe this guy or someone similar. I am not sure. Maybe he knows someone." Then quite abruptly she changed the subject. "Have you checked in yet?" she asked. We confirmed that we hadn't. "I will just call the office to say I am helping you check in and then I will go with you to the Gurko." We made no further enquiry. At the Gurko Hotel we checked in. They all spoke perfect English so we could have managed without Desi. We dossed our bags and sat in the bar with three beers. It seemed a better idea than coffee. Desi took her mobile out of her bag. "I am calling a friend." She stated simply.

Ten minutes later an enormous old Mercedes, the model that one used to see in Germany in the late seventies and eighties drew up outside. A huge man in his forties stepped from the car. As he shut the car door the engine, already switched off, gave one last spasm before it finally fell silent. The guy who we soon knew as Nicky looked behind him as if the noise had been an indiscretion on his part. He stepped forward and Desi introduced us to each other. Nicky did not speak a word of English, but Desi explained that his wife, Dima would soon be joining us and that she spoke excellent English. Despite his lack of English Nicky seemed to understand perfectly when I asked if he wanted a beer and confusingly shook his head which to a Bulgarian usually means yes. I wasn't absolutely sure, but ordered him a beer anyway. Buying him a beer that he did not want seemed better than the alternative. Once received, he downed half of it in one suck so it seemed I had got it right.

Nicky was the sort of guy that you would recognise as a builder anywhere in the world: big belly, dusty hair, black tee shirt, hard-wearing dark trousers, large grimy boots and hands like shovels. He even sported a builder's bum so there could be no doubt as to his profession. He was to us both a reassuring sight. This was going to turn out well. Within minutes Nicky's other half arrived and the contrast could not have been more marked. The girl that Desi introduced as her best friend was at least fifteen years younger than Nicky. Dima was a pretty young woman with a lovely smile, intelligent eyes and short cropped dark hair; the sort of girl that any guy would not hesitate to introduce to his mum. Also as Desi had promised her English, although less spontaneous than Desi's, was flawless. In terms of getting business from Brits wanting building work they were I thought a winning combination. Desi gave Nicky and Dima a rundown of what we were seeking and then took her leave. Understandably she seemed anxious to get back to her office. As far as we were concerned she had kept her side of the unspoken bargain.

Very soon we were back in the little house in Gurko Street only this time our builder had plenty to say. Each time we explained what we wanted and Dima had translated he came back with counter suggestions that were inevitably better thought out than our ideas. Half way round we bowed to the inevitable and simply said that as long as it had a bathroom, kitchen, living space and some bedrooms we would leave it up to him. So for the rest of the time we were there he did all the talking and we were amazed how Dima could translate all the building terms as easily as if she had translating an order in a restaurant. When we were finished Dima suggested we went for a few beers, a girl after our own heart. She said that Nicky wanted to take us to their local and we happily agreed. When we got there I was delighted to see that their local was the little bar overlooking the town that Marieluise and I had dubbed the 'Cave'. We ordered the beers and while Tony, Dima and I drank and chatted Nicky worked with a pencil on the back of Dima's fag packet. After twenty minutes he was ready to make his announcement, but much as we wanted to hear the estimated price he would not be hurried. Nicky spent another twenty minutes telling us through Dima, who translated with patience and skill, exactly what he was proposing. The price – he was clear that it was not an estimate – was thirty eight thousand leva, about nineteen thousand Euros; a cool twelve thousand Euros cheaper than the other man's estimate.

On Tony's insistence we told Nicky that we needed to speak together for a moment on our own which he seemed fine about. We got up and walked to a bar on the other side of the small alleyway. "Why are we here?" I enquired immediately. "Surely we are going to take it." "Of course we bloody are!" said Tony, "But there's no need for him to realise how keen we are, otherwise next time it will be more. So order a couple of beers and take your time."

I have never seen Tony take so long over a pint, but when we eventually returned to Nicky and Dima they were deep in conversation and hardly seemed to have missed us. As had been agreed Tony asked several 'clarification' questions which Nicky and Dima answered with care and patience. Eventually Tony ordered four more beers and said yes, Nicky could go ahead. We toasted our deal and sat on at the Cave for several hours. We really enjoyed each other's company and it was already becoming clear that we would become friends rather than just people who did business together.

2006: Renovations; Flourishing Friendships

Thursday 14th September 2006

Tony and his wife Kay had been out earlier in the summer and as with Marieluise and me the previous year they had bought a small house in the old town which, like the property in Gurko Street, was in need of renovation. Now that we had three apartments rented out in Varna and a couple of properties in Veliko Tarnovo there was quite a lot of business to conduct so today we arrived in Varna again on a 'package tour' to Golden Sands. Last time we had been very lucky with our hotel, this time not so lucky. We were booked into a high rise utilitarian hotel. It was very old and quite shabby. The breakfast was terrible, so terrible it made us laugh for the first few mornings. Later we just got up and headed elsewhere for breakfast. When we discovered how old the hotel was, everything fell into place. It probably had not seen renovations since the Soviet era. Were we bothered? Not one bit. The beds were clean and comfortable enough. We were not on holiday and we could afford to eat elsewhere. Anyway as Tony said the group back home whose money we were investing could hardly complain that we had been extravagant. The hotel's saving grace was that it was dirt cheap.

It had been quite late when we arrived and so we had a few beers, a plate of chips and hit the sack. As usual we had a series of appointments on the following day which included seeing our rental agent from Address, the redoubtable Ivo. We needed to be fresh and alert.

Friday 15th September 2006

The business in Varna was soon conducted. Our first visit was to Rada and as always it was lovely to see her. Our business has now reached the point where we need an accountant and Rada had invited a guy named Peter to introduce him to us. Our response to the question of whether we wanted to take him on was a simple one: If Rada was recommending him then that was fine by us. Again we were reminded how at sea you could be in such situations if you did not have people like Rada that you could trust and completely rely on. Just how would you find someone to conduct your financial affairs otherwise? It would be fraught with danger and risk. Had we been lucky? To some extent we had, but we have always had a plan which we have kept to and as well as that we have been extremely careful.

Next we went to see Georgi to get an up to date valuation on the properties and to generally find out how solid our investments have been. All reports were positive, but Tony and I both know that we will only really get an answer to that when we come to try and sell the apartments. That is a long time off, but it is good to know that even at this early stage things seem to be moving in the right direction. It will turn out to have been a wise move to buy city apartments rather than holiday properties as the tourist market is always likely to be quite volatile. Since our first visit two and a half years ago there have been big changes in Bulgaria almost all of them positive, but we have noticed that most of the progress has been in the big cities with rural areas so far seeing little significant change. Varna in particular has seen a lot of changes. Tony and I felt quite satisfied and we will be able to give a positive message to our friends when we get home.

When Tony was here with his wife Kay he saw that Georgi had bought himself a little car of which he was immensely proud. Best of all from Georgi's point of view the car had a CD player. However it was still difficult to get hold of the music he wanted and Tony had noted this with interest. He had obviously also asked Georgi in some detail what type of music he liked, because out of his bag he suddenly produced about twenty CDs. Not a single one of the artists were known to me, but Georgi went into raptures as he rifled through the stack smiling over each one. Georgi was completely overwhelmed not only by Tony's generosity, but more so by the fact that he had gone to such trouble for Georgi's benefit. To me it was no surprise. The Tony I know takes enormous pleasure from making people happy and I have seen gestures like this from him on many occasions. As always Tony brushed the thanks aside, slightly embarrassed by the fuss.

Our next appointment was with someone who Tony was never likely to treat in a similar way. Ivo joined us, hair slicked back and smile in place and gave us the normal tale about the different items that had eaten in to our expected profits from the three rentals. We had long since decided that we could do little about this and maybe they were all legitimate. The rentals easily pay for us to run the business without using up any of our capital and that is fine. Funny how we so like our other partners, Rada, Georgi, Desi and of course Nicky and Dima, but the only one who seems desperate to be our friend, i.e. Ivo, we cannot take to.

After a quick visit to the bank to check the health of our account that was our business in Varna completed. After so many hectic trips we had decided that this time we were going to enjoy our time in and around Varna and that of course necessitated a trip to our old haunt, the Fox in Varna.

To say the landlord was pleased to see us was an understatement. The locals who frequent his tavern are not well off and they usually languish for hours over one drink and so although his bar is usually quite full it does not mean that his takings are high. Therefore to have two customers who drink at a fair pace and also order a great deal of food makes a great difference to him. If he has the promise that it might go on for several days then he will see a real difference in his profits. That is almost certainly one reason why he likes to see us and gives us such a warm welcome. I also believe that he feels different about his bar when some foreigners are drinking there as if by our presence we make the place more cosmopolitan. There is also just a chance that he might like us.

Soon the 'interpreter' was sitting at our table and the whole experience started to take on a pleasantly familiar feel. The interpreter drinks either Rakia or white wine. If he is on wine he always drinks the house white, usually by the glass. As he regarded our arrival as a special occasion and also because he was now expecting a longer shift than normal, he decided to order a carafe. Tony was at that time drinking house red and apparently had the only carafe in the landlord's stock. As a result the interpreter's wine arrived in a 500ml spring water bottle. He started to complain, but the landlord cut him short. I asked him in German what the landlord had said and he replied that the landlord had told him in no uncertain terms that when he learned to drink wine like Tony he would be welcome to the only carafe! He did not seem in the least put out. After a pleasant evening we made our way to the taxi rank to get a fare back to Golden Sands. The driver charged us twenty five leva and we did not turn a hair.

When we got back to the resort at about eleven thirty the place was still buzzing. When it comes to having one last beer we make no claims to having strong willpower. There was fun to be had and we were more than easily seduced. We decided that some music would be good and as we walked through the resort we could hear various offerings, but our attention was caught by a rendition of Tears of Heaven, the Eric Clapton classic not very far away. We headed in the direction of the sound and as we turned a corner we could see and hear a young guy making a decent job of the guitar solo. If anything he was elaborating the original. He was a very nice looking young man and he was positioned right out front of one of the top bars. He was attracting quite a lot of attention and we could observe a number of the women dragging their husbands/partners towards the vacant seats close to where he was playing. Tony and I also sat down in the same area although our interest was strictly music and beer. After the taxi journey I needed to visit the loo and so headed into the bar. As I walked past the artist the vocals began again and I could have sworn he was miming. I assumed I was mistaken and thought no more about it until I reached the inside of the bar. I could not find the loo and so probably wandered into parts of the building where I was not supposed to go. As I passed a dark corner I saw an old guy of about seventy playing a keyboard and singing into a large microphone doing an excellent job of...Tears of Heaven.

Sunday 17th September 2006

We had spent the evenings of Thursday and Friday in a similar way: eating and drinking at the Fox in Varna and then returning to the resort for some music and a nightcap. We had intended to do the same on Saturday, but did not have the energy to travel into Varna and so we stayed at the resort and had a relatively quiet night. Today we were taking the bus to Veliko Tarnovo as we had some interesting business there. We would have a chance to see what sort of a job Nicky had done renovating the house on Gurko Street and on the basis of that we would decide whether to engage him to do a similar job on the house that Tony had bought earlier in the year. We took a taxi into the city, but asked the driver to drop us near the Fox in Varna so that we could say goodbye. As we approached we could see a man in overalls descending a ladder that was propped against the outside wall of our favourite hostelry. The landlord along with several locals including the interpreter were gazing up admiring the man's work. The landlord had paid for the front of the building including the windows and front door to be completely repainted and in places re-rendered. The man had even painted a new name board over the door, although we were still not able to ascertain the real name of the place. Anyway we were happy with the title we had conferred. The landlord saw us coming and beckoned us over. He was beaming with pride and in perfect English he proclaimed that his bar was now "Very European."

The interpreter explained that the landlord had been wanting to have the place painted for more than a year and had taken the opportunity from the extra cash he had earned from us. The painter had started the work right away on Saturday morning and had just finished. The interpreter confided that the landlord had wobbled a little when we did not turn up on Saturday night because he had based his calculations on the assumption that he would have three night's earnings from us. However, he had just about had enough to pay the bill so all was well. The pride on the landlord's face made Tony and I feel quite proud of our contribution. It just goes to show how much good can be done by two nights of debauchery.

The bus journeys that we now took frequently were usually uneventful. The buses were almost always full given car ownership was still very low and bus travel was very cheap indeed. The journey between Varna and Veliko Tarnovo took about three hours. On this particular trip there was a group of lads a bit the worst for wear sitting in the seats in front of us. They were very loud and getting on everybody's nerves. I was sitting directly behind a particularly boisterous member of the group trying to read. Every few minutes he messed about with his seat adjustment and the seat came within inches of the book I was reading. It was beginning to really irritate me. I gave him a few hard looks, but he did not take the hint. When the seat flew back for the umpteenth time and knocked the book clean out of my hands I saw red. I leaned forward grabbed his seat adjustment lever and thrust the seat and him forward with a real jerk. The next thing the whole group was staring menacingly at me. Tony as always kept his cool. As he turned to address me I was expecting words of solidarity. "That was clever." he said. "There are six of them.......and only one of you!"

The bus trundled into Veliko Tarnovo without further incident arriving at about six thirty. As was now our custom we went across to the Humphrey Bogart bar for a few pints of Zagorka. After that we made our way to the Gurko Hotel where we checked in and went down to the restaurant for something to eat. It had been a long day and Nicky and Dima were meeting us in the hotel lobby at nine the following morning. We were in bed by eleven and asleep by five past.

Monday 18th September 2006

Nicky and Dima arrived at just after nine. We had resisted the temptation to look at the house last night, although of course it had a new door and lock and so we would only have been able to view it from the outside. When we told Nicky this he was both surprised and pleased. He told us that the house was finished and he hoped we would like it. With a twinkle in his eye he informed us that not all the renovations had been done in the way we had agreed. We were not fazed by this news as we were confident that any changes would be positive ones. We walked together from the hotel. As I have indicated previously, the outside of the house gives no indication of how unusual it is inside. The exterior had been sympathetically renovated, but it was the inside that we were anxious to see and that Nicky was keen to show us.

An example of Nicky's internal renovations at 34 Gurko Street

Gurko Street from the river side

When we saw the place it was difficult to remember what it had looked like previously. Nicky had turned a complete wreckage into a charming little house. The work was of an extremely high standard and Nicky had managed to completely modernise the house whilst maintaining its unusual character. We were very pleased indeed and as promised the price he quoted was the price he was charging. We complimented Nicky on his work and proceeded at once to our other house in Tunel Street to ask him to repeat his magic there. The price he quoted was virtually the same as for Gurko Street and we happily agreed for him to go ahead. Our expectation was that we would return the following summer to find our second little house in Veliko Tarnovo renovated to the same standard. Our portfolio of properties was starting to look quite interesting. Again we could look forward to going home and getting our friends and investors together for another positive report. That evening we again enjoyed a few beers with Dima and Nicky and we were also joined by Desi who was a lot of fun. Friendships that were to become central to my later adventures in Bulgaria were now flourishing.

2014: Settling In

Monday 14th April 2014

We have now been here over a week and the time has flown. We have tried to just rest up and acclimatise ourselves to a different way of life. We are also giving the horses time to do the same. Doing nothing is not in our nature and Marieluise in particular finds it hard when there is clearly so much to do. Their royal highnesses – the horses – have settled in incredibly well and I am still in wonder at how they managed the journey. They were simply brilliant and except when they disappeared, which was clearly not their fault or intention, they have caused us very little anxiety. So after such an epic undertaking we all need a rest and even at the end of a day of doing little more than the necessary chores we both feel tired. In any event we will have to get used to a slower pace of life because in Bulgaria nothing happens quickly and there is nothing you can do to shake things up. Having done business here for ten years I am used to this and have become fairly accepting of it, though not entirely. Marieluise on the other hand finds it almost against nature to wait for things so she has much more adjustment to make.

Our horses resting up in their new home

So in terms of getting used to a slower pace we were presented with a perfect role model by the arrival of Nicky and his workmen to finish off the work on the fields. The stables are, thank God, largely completed and as the good builder he is, Nicky has yet again done a great job. Their day started briskly arriving on site at ten to ten and then taking twenty minutes to get their work clothes on and get their tools together. So at quarter past ten they finally lumbered into action. I take my hat off to them. I was not aware the human body could move so slowly without shutting down. I found it amusing. Marieluise on the other hand was speechless. Nicky, in the role of non-working supervisor, uncovered an armchair that he had apparently covered in plastic the last time they were here and sat down in a spot from which he could observe the whole proceedings without any fear of getting involved in the actual work. He is after all the boss and this status obviously carries with it certain advantages. The work that remained to be finished was fencing off one more paddock. We soon learned that the holes had already been made and the posts were about to be delivered.

As anticipated, within ten minutes a lorry came crawling up the hill. Its arrival was preceded by a huge plume of black smoke. This finally cleared to reveal a nineteen thirties vintage tipper truck with a huge menacing radiator grill. I have honestly only seen such a thing in films. Even when I was a child the trucks were more modern than this. It drove past the iron gates that form the entrance to the field and with much hullaballoo proceeded to back into the field. Unfortunately for the driver he had many experts on hand to supervise his reversing manoeuvre with the result that he twice backed into the concrete posts. It was a close thing, but the old posts proved more solid than the lorry and various miscellaneous bits fell off the truck. The truck driver got out to examine the damage and, apparently deciding that the bits that had dropped off served no useful purpose of which he was aware, climbed back into the cab to repeat the manoeuvre.

At this moment Nicky rose like the Kraken waking from his chair to do his duty and ensure the lorry reversed successfully through the gates into the field. He waved his men aside and the lorry towards him with a series of gestures which were not meant to be ignored. The driver looked doubtful but Nicky confidently directed him backwards. His aim for the gate was true, but he was taking the drive wheels of the truck through thick mud and inevitably the wheels began to spin. Unperturbed Nicky waved him on and soon the truck, Nicky and his entire workforce were lost in a cloud of black smoke and flying mud. I could hear further bits and pieces falling off the truck, but this time I believe it was caused by the sheer exertion of the old wagon. Suddenly the spinning stopped the wheels having gone deep enough to locate rock or at least dry ground and the truck lurched backwards into the field. The engine cut out and the vehicle came to an immediate halt. As the smoke cleared I witnessed a scene of contentment. From everyone's point of view the wagon had been successfully directed into the field without incident and the cargo could now be unloaded on site so as to prevent any unnecessary carrying. The driver, who I thought would be stressed beyond endurance was a picture of tranquillity and now began the operation of tipping his load. As the "posts and rails" tumbled out I realised that they were not posts and rails in the sense that I imagined, but a pile of pine tree trunks, bark and all.

The Lorry trundled off to perform its next mission impossible. From this point on I was able to witness the "Lost Boys" as we had now christened Nicky's workers ply their primitive trade. With a set of tools that might have impressed someone from the Iron Age but which would surely shame even a pre-war tradesman they set about scraping off the bark. I now observed that the different members of the team worked at different speeds and also that this was tolerated, I think on the grounds of seniority. Certainly the youngest amongst them worked considerably quicker than his older workmates, but this attracted not admiration, but rather smug looks indicating he would soon either revert to a more sensible pace or burn himself out completely. After a gruelling day, work terminated at ten minutes to three, the Lost Boys changed back into their town garb and the whole crew departed. I went to check progress to discover nine peeled tree trunks represented a good day's work for five men. How long was this going to take?

Tuesday 15th April 2014

The lost boys arrived earlier today, about twenty to ten, looking like they could have a day's work in them. By ten they were hard at it, again engaged in scraping the bark off what was eventually to be posts and rails. Nicky, seated comfortably in the armchair left by the old lady who previously lived here, gave off an air of authority following his heroics with the tipper truck yesterday. The youngest member of the lost boys was again leading the way, only this time, under Nicky's expectant gaze, his workmates seemed to be responding positively to the example he was setting.

Last week I had complied with the ultimatum from the car park impresario to move the horsebox, by driving it up to the centre of Todorcheta where it now stood. Unfortunately the centre of the village is little more than a junction where the track up the hill splits off into two tracks that lead up and down to the fifteen or so houses that make up the little hamlet. The horsebox was now dominating this area and although cars could pass easily it was not acceptable as a long or even medium term solution. Having said that nobody was complaining and the lady living right by where I had parked – "the lady from Varna" – was at pains to assure me it was "ne problem". I had put pressure on myself by sticking a sign in the windscreen in Bulgarian to say it would be moved inside a week. D-day was approaching fast. Although the presence of the horsebox caused no animosity it became a big talking point in the village and everyone had an opinion as to what was the best solution.

The "Lady from Varna" led the liberal wing advocating that it should stay where it was and that any pressure to move it was a hostile act inconsistent with Bulgarian hospitality and the overwhelming need to make us welcome. Gencho, an influential member of the village, offered a spot next to where his car was parked although this was common land and not his to allocate. In addition it was steep and slippery in wet weather, unlike the flat spot where he parked his car that would have been perfect. I favoured hiring a digger and carving out a flat parking space next to our house, but our nearest neighbour, Plamen, thought this would affect the bedrock that his garden was built on with possible disastrous results. I thought this highly unlikely, but kept this opinion to myself and respected his right to object. The last thing we wanted to do was to upset our next door neighbours. Nicky, our builder, still flushed with his success at reversing the tipper truck into the iron gates opposite the house was adamant that just inside the gates would be the perfect parking spot in terms of security and convenience. All we needed to do, he maintained, was widen the entrance by knocking down one of the concrete posts, already loosened by the lorry, and making a new post and an extra section for the metal gate. It is always difficult to argue with Nicky, but I now know the horse wagon well and it is far too long to do this manoeuvre successfully. On top of that I have noticed that whenever it rains all the water gathers just inside this gate.

As I pursued this conversation with Nicky all work stopped so that the lost boys could form their own opinions and no doubt at some point express them in the sort of half language and half action form of communication we had adopted between us. Also listening in were Honeyman and his elderly father who were apparently the men of action within the village, because no sooner had Nicky made his pronouncement they started dismantling the gate. It was not easy persuading them to stop.

A long set of wrangling negotiations ensued. During this process the youngest lost boy suddenly showed his true colours as a reasonably able interpreter, although given he had learned his English from video games the phrases exchanged were sometimes more alarming than I would have liked. Eventually a deal was struck. I would get my way and an area for the lorry would be carved out next to our house, only the work would be done by hand and the job would be entrusted to the lost boys so as to minimise the danger of Plamen's garden collapsing. Plamen graciously accepted the compromise and it was agreed that the lost boys would be diverted from post making and would make a start on the lorry park the very next day. The whole fraught matter had been successfully resolved, but the long negotiations had taken their toll on the lost boys and work ended for the day at two twenty five. As they left I went to inspect their work hoping that the early promise had been converted into posts and rails. Alas all I found was a slightly bigger pile of tree trunks minus their bark.

Wednesday 16th April 2014

Early this morning we had quite a bit of rain, but it stopped by half past seven and the sun was just showing itself from behind the clouds when the phone rang. It was Dima passing a message from Nicky that he and the lost boys would not be coming to Todorcheta today due to the weather. I know Bulgarian workers well and was not surprised, although I had hoped that the excitement of starting on the lorry park project might have motivated them. More likely they had now had time to consider what this new project entailed. The prospect of hacking away at solid rock with primitive tools was bad enough, but with the added fear that they may be rained on, it proved too much to endure.

However, Nicky had an alternative suggestion. We had been telling Nicky and Dima that we urgently needed bedding for the stables, either straw or wood shavings. He had spoken to the proprietor of a wood yard in Veliko Tarnovo that he often used and had been told that he had some shavings that we were welcome to for a small charge. Also his mother was a member of her village cooperative and had been given her allocation of straw for which she had no use. We were welcome to this as well. This would mean me getting the lorry back on the road and the distances involved were considerable. However, because we have only been here a week or so we remain largely dependent on Nicky to resolve such matters for us and, given he lives and works in Veliko Tarnovo his solutions inevitably take us in that direction.

Rather optimistically, given what we were undertaking Nicky said we should meet him at the wood yard in forty five minutes. The directions were duly given using bars in VT as the landmarks and as soon as we could, we set off. Given the apparent urgency we had no time to purchase a vinetka, Bulgarian road tax, and had to undertake the first half of our journey without one until we got to the next town, Dryanovo, where it was possible to buy one. Sods law, I passed two parked police cars on this short journey, but made it to Dryanovo without being arrested. We continued towards VT, entering the town forty minutes behind the schedule Nicky had set for us. Marieluise was amazed at how easily I found the wood yard and even more amazed at the number of bars I had drunk in.

If Nicky had not been standing there I would never have realised that I had arrived at a wood yard. The entrance was a hole in the wall and I was informed by way of explanation that it had previously been a Turkish bath although this to me just made the place more confusing. I had no further time for reflection, because at that moment I noticed some activity at the entrance and the oldest member of the lost boys, the Professor, emerged from the hole in the wall carrying a plastic sack that presumably contained wood shavings. Shortly afterwards the next three lost boys emerged, each carrying an identical sack. So Nicky had employed the lost boys to do the carrying, although we had tried to tell him that at home we did everything ourselves and did not employ people for such tasks. Nevertheless I was at least encouraged that this must be a sign that there was quite a lot of shavings to collect. Immediately Marieluise and I set to, taking the sacks from the lost boys as they emerged from the hole in the side of the Turkish bath. Nicky intervened at once with gestures that inferred you do not have a dog and bark yourself. The lost boys had been employed to carry bags and that is how it should be done.

To add to our frustration when twenty six very loosely filled bags had been deposited in the lorry the job was done. That was it. Nicky had anticipated a lot more, but someone else had beaten us to it. However, we were yet to collect the straw from Nicky's mother. I now proceeded to drive to the village of Nicky's birth, forty kilometres away on the road to Elena, to collect sixteen bales of straw. Obviously I did not know the way and one of the lost boys, the history man was allocated to me as a guide. So Marieluise, the history man and I climbed into the cab and set off in the direction of Elena. Nicky and the remaining lost boys drove off in Nicky's Mercedes presumably finished for the day.

I followed the history man's non-verbal signals and after forty minutes and two wrong turns we arrived at the home of Nicky's mother; and there to meet us to help us load the sixteen bales of straw were the three remaining lost boys. Needless to say the task was soon completed and I approached Nicky to settle up. The straw was of no use to his mother and that was a very kind gift from her. The guy at the saw mill wanted just ten leva for the shavings. So in the end I had to pay half a day's wages to four men to load bedding to the value of ten leva – about four pounds. We were grateful to Nicky because now we had bedding and at this stage we had no means of finding it ourselves. However, somehow we needed to get across to him that our funds were not endless or realistically we needed to start sorting things for ourselves. We paid up, gave him a box of chocolates for his mother and put the whole episode down to experience. Still I had no complaints. As usual Nicky had sorted the problem.

Thursday 17th April 2014

Today the sun was shining and at just before ten Nicky's car transporting the lost boys could be heard labouring up the hill. Work clothes on and tools in hand they approached the job and I have to say that in just a few hours they had made a real impression on the slope which was already looking more level and was starting to resemble a parking space. I was just starting to believe I had underestimated them when work came to an abrupt halt. It was only one in the afternoon, but tomorrow was Good Friday. As far as Nicky and his team were concerned it was now "the holidays".

However, later that day I started to reflect on the whole issue of work and particularly how work was viewed by Bulgarians and by the British. Like most of the western world Brits hold work in high esteem and firmly believe that you get things in life by hard work. That can prove to be true, but equally there are plenty of people at home who work hard all their lives for scant rewards. The Bulgarians attitude to work is very different. A few days ago I came across a small book written by a local man, Velizar Velchev, from the nearby village of Boriki. The book is called '7/8 The British Way' and touches on this issue. He quotes some Bulgarian sayings about work, some of which are quite categorical: "Work is *not* to be praised" and the more prosaic "Work gives one not wealth but a humpback". My favourite is the exact opposite of the British saying ""Don't put off until tomorrow what you can do today": "Work is not a hare – it won't run away".

Who is right? When I listen to the British people who live in Bulgaria the most common complaint I hear is that the Bulgarians don't like to work. I catch myself saying this especially when I want to get things done. However, when you ask the same people what it is they most like about Bulgaria they inevitably make some reference to the slower pace of life. Looking at my neighbours and Bulgarian friends they certainly do not have monetary wealth, but their life is rich. They do the work they need to do to put food on the table and a roof over their heads. They live and work in a beautiful country with wonderful weather. They work neither in the pouring rain nor the boiling sun. They love to sit and chat. They love their families and spend a lot of time with them. They treasure their holidays together. They laugh a lot. Who is to say they are not wealthy.

Easter Sunday 20th April 2014

Today we decided that the horses had been given long enough to rest up and it was time for them to get some exercise. We groomed them and saddled them up and set off at about ten in the morning. We rode down to the centre of the village and took the only other fork that leads downwards to about half a dozen houses. We passed Gencho's on the left and a further house on the right that seems to house the only unfriendly family in the small village. The outside of the house has recently been partially renovated, but the area surrounding the house including the garden is a complete tip. From what one can see through the grimy windows the interior of the house is no better. At the end of this road is a newly created mansion owned by a clothes entrepreneur from Ruse. The house has been renovated by Nicky after the Ruse businessman noticed the quality of his work on our house. The owner is obviously, like most Bulgarians, very security conscious and on his instructions Nicky has erected an enormous stone wall that surrounds the whole house and grounds.

Here the road ends and a path through the forest begins. We took this path and were quickly engulfed in the depths of the woods. The path is magnificent, although fairly overgrown and as we have been told it was for many years used by villagers to walk to the train. Use of the train by people from Todorcheta has been superseded by cars and buses, but as we discovered when we emerged out the far end of the path the old halt is still there, although quite dilapidated. However, the railway line itself from Gabrovo to Tsareva Livada is still very much in use and connects the Gabrovo area to the main North to South European railway line CE 95. This line also passes through Dryanovo and Tryavna.

From the end of the path we were able to discover a number of very small villages and after riding a loop through several of these we returned via the forest path onto the lower road of our village, Todorcheta. As we rode along this path the old guy from the house that looks like a tip emerged to point to a pile of horse droppings that he wanted us to remove. Marieluise intentionally misunderstood him and agreed he could take them for his garden. He was not amused and half an hour later I returned with a shovel to remove the horse poo from all the other rubbish surrounding his house. At this stage I just want to keep the peace.

Just around the corner going up the hill to our house we were confronted by about eight goats under the charge of a wizened, bent old goat lady. I do not think either of our horses had ever seen a goat up close before and we were not sure how they would feel about passing them. We need not have worried. The goat lady stepped aside and disappeared into the bushes. To our amazement she then rang a little cowbell and all the goats obediently followed her and they all disappeared as quickly as they had materialised. On making enquiries later we found out that she was a self-employed goat shepherd who minds people's goats at a daily charge of one lev (about forty pence) per goat. We have seen her many times since during rides and walks turning up almost anywhere.

Tuesday 22nd April 2014

Well today was a really fruitful day in terms of getting ourselves settled and organised. Our vet, Momchil had put us in touch with a farmer, living only about five miles away, who could provide us with hay. Using Momchil as an intermediary we had ordered a hundred bales, fifty to be collected today and fifty next week. Back home I would have simply done two runs and collected the hundred bales in one day, but it is all a bit different now. The first problem is I am not completely clear where I am going to store the hay including the stuff I am getting today. So in typical Bulgarian style, I put off the second collection for a week or so to give me time to think.

The first thing I had to do was drive in the car to Gabrovo, the nearest town, to buy a vignette. This is Bulgarian road tax which for a lorry is very expensive. Luckily enough you only need it to drive and not to park and also you can buy it for a day, a week, a month, or a year. Having been told by a not entirely sound source that it costs eight hundred leva for a year – about three hundred and thirty pounds – I have plumped for a daily ticket at twenty leva a hit. Given this was the third vignette I had purchased I made a note to self to work out the economics of this. Knowing what passes for logic in Bulgaria, I would not be surprised to find out that it costs twenty five leva for a month.

So with vignette stuck to the windscreen, along with the other two that are impossible to remove, we fired up the wagon yet again and headed in pursuit of hay. As I was driving it struck me that if I continued with the policy of daily vignettes I would soon not be able to see out of the windscreen. Still that is for another day. Most of the drive to Dumnitsi was along one of those roads quite common in Bulgaria that seem to have been built for a surge of traffic that never materialised. It is a vast highway heading in the direction of a fairly inauspicious town called Sevlievo. All along the route it proclaims the European Union as the source of funding. It might be more sensible to keep this quiet. Anyway, given we were in a large vehicle it was nice to find that we were the only people driving either to or from Sevlievo that day, or do they know an even bigger road? Suffice to say that we arrived at the entrance to the village unimpeded by other vehicles and before we had a chance to find our bearings, a farmer popped up in the middle of the main road through Dumnitsi and waved us towards him.

It soon became apparent that he wanted me to back into some reasonably wide grey gates which I managed comfortably. He then intended me to back quite a long way into the narrow yard past impediments like an enormous disused oil tank and an ancient septic tank that seemed to have half surfaced from the hole in which it was originally buried. This left at times about two inches on either side of the wagon. Now Marieluise has very efficiently and successfully guided me forwards and backwards past all sorts of impediments and in and out of some very tight spots all over Europe. As a result I have generally adopted a policy of only taking guidance from her. However, it soon became evident that this guy knew what he was about and had obviously done this very job in this yard many times before. I therefore rather brutally dispensed with Marieluise's loyal services and took my directions from Sabi. There was more to come. The next obstacle was an overhanging roof that the lorry would not pass under and so I had to continue wide of the roof into a narrow passage remaining completely straight. To think that just over a month ago I was in trepidation of turning the lorry round in Richie's enormous and fairly flat yard. The final hazard was the mains electricity cable to the house that hung limply across the yard at a height about twelve inches lower than the wagon. Sabi was on the case. With a very long pole lying nearby for just this purpose he gently lifted the cable over the wagon.

I could not see this action clearly and remember thinking I hope the pole isn't made of metal.

Then abruptly he ordered me to halt. Almost before I was out of the wagon he had lowered the ramp, but not to the floor. With a thick beam of wood placed on end below the ramp he ensured that it came down only so far as to form a floor on exactly the same level as the empty inside of the truck. He jumped aboard his platform and invited me to join him at which point unseen hands started dropping bales of hay from above onto the ramp cum platform with perfect precision. I stood for a moment in awe, but soon with friendly yet firm gestures Sabi indicated that as owner of the transport packing was my job. This was the most efficient collection of fifty bales of hay I have ever witnessed or been part of. Within minutes the job was done and the hay paid for.

Now work completed, Sabi and his overhead accomplice went into hospitality mode. They each gave the widest of grins and shook my hand firmly with a laudable attempt at the English word "Welcome". Before Marieluise they virtually bowed and shook her hand for almost a minute. Next they took us to see their own horses which were beautiful Friesians, loved and well-kept and obviously well used to being affectionately handled. They then went and fetched the horses' passport and family tree, shouting "pedigree; pedigree." Marieluise looked at what they showed her with great respect and they seemed delighted to have made the point that they were serious horse owners, which they obviously were. After all the stories you hear about Bulgarians never having a positive relationship with horses this was lovely to see.

By this time two neighbours had joined the throng and all four of them were excitedly chatting to us in their native tongue and, although I have been studiously applying myself to learning the language, I understood not a word. It was a very warm day and given I had been loading hay bales above my head I was a sweaty and itchy mess. Sabi seeing this led me to an outside sink and hung a freshly laundered towel on a nail hammered into a nearby vine for that purpose. He indicated I should remove my shirt and have a good wash which I proceeded to do. On the wooden draining board beside the sink were three items: a bar of soap, a lettuce about to be washed and a slab of goat's cheese. Welcome to the real Bulgaria.

Washed and refreshed I returned to the ever more animated group, upon which Sabi appeared from the house with a huge bottle of juice, crystal water glasses from the nineteenth century and an enormous unopened box of chocolates. After expertly removing the cellophane he handed them round the group, with a demeanour that indicated to his neighbours that they were expected to take one each with six or more intended for each for us. We bravely played our part, although Marieluise is usually queasy after just two or three chocolates. These were lovely people and I was glad that I had decided to make another trip of it the following week. Except for backing into Sabi's yard again I will look forward to it immensely. We said our goodbyes and returned to the highway to heaven with a warm glow.

Wednesday 23rd April 2014

Today the warm glow lost some of its lustre when on unloading the hay we discovered we were three bales short. We were disappointed and we had a long debate about whether or not this was accidental, given how incongruous it was alongside the marvellous hospitality we were shown. Marieluise got it right when she said that there was not a chance in hell that we would have got home and found we had three too many. This was absolutely true and yet it was also true that the welcome and hospitality were completely genuine and in no way a cover for short changing us. To our Bulgarian friends the two things were quite separate. They had intentionally given us three bales too few and this was just another example of what they regarded as good business. In my experience, which is quite extensive, Bulgarians have no business acumen whatsoever. By making twelve leva on the deal they put at risk ever having us as customers again. And what good customers we are. It is a rare event indeed for a Bulgarian farmer to sell four hundred leva worth of hay to one customer in one hit with the added advantage that the customer collects it himself and pays on the nail in new notes. We had already told them that we wanted another hundred bales as soon as they cut new hay in June. If I did not have such a deep seated natural empathy for them I would certainly have gone elsewhere for the new hay. At home if John who I buy from is uncertain about the number he would simply throw in two more to be sure. And what is the result? I never go to anyone else and before we left home I gave him three hundred and twenty pounds to provide hay for Max, the horse we left at home, although the hay I was paying for hadn't even been grown let alone cut. Well they won't sell me short again.

2007: The Birthday Party
Wednesday 13th June 2007

It is now more than three years since our first visit to Bulgaria and the changes that have taken place have been remarkable. On 29th March 2004, just days before our first visit, Bulgaria formally became a member of NATO. Now on 1st January this year they have become a full member of the European Union. They have been pursuing this for a decade or more. In the lead up to accession the EU has spent a considerable amount of money on improving the infrastructure of Bulgaria and the changes can be seen everywhere. However, the reports during this accession period highlighted the need for further efforts to fight against political corruption and organized crime. Although they have made some progress in these areas there is still a long way to go. There is still a big difference between civic life in Bulgaria and within western European countries. Corruption and obstructive bureaucracy were commonplace in Communist Bulgaria and it would appear that they remain a problem in civic and political life here. There also remains an overwhelming distrust of the political system and even more worrying is the deep seated distrust that often seems to exist between fellow citizens. Until these things are eradicated changes in the infrastructure and economic progress will not lead to Bulgaria being at ease with itself. Some young people I have met believe real change will only happen when the current civic and political leaders give way to the next generation. I think they could be right.

Understandably Bulgaria and its people are focused on economic improvement and slowly but surely this is happening for them. There will no doubt be an acceleration as a direct result of EU membership. However, it is not just about becoming richer economically. Bulgaria has a rich cultural history and proud sporting traditions and these things also need nurturing. This is a dangerous area for a westerner to comment on. As western Europeans venture into Bulgaria the relative wealth of its citizens is plain to see for Bulgarians and inevitably they want some of that for themselves. In that process I hope they can retain some of the things that make it such an attractive country: the natural beauty of Bulgaria, the incredible hospitality of its people, their love of family and of relaxing and celebrating as a family. Sometimes when I am wanting to get things done the pace of life here can drive me mad, but that is *my* problem. I hope they manage to keep things that way.

So here we are again, needing to get less done than on previous visits and more able to relax and enjoy that slower pace of life. We have some business to conduct in Varna, but things are increasingly taking care of themselves. So if we want to enjoy what Bulgaria has to offer we need to head for Veliko Tarnovo and to spend some time with our dear friends, Nicky and Dima. That indeed is our plan. We have already been in touch with Dima and learned that Friday the fifteenth is her thirtieth birthday and she is to have a small party to which we are cordially invited. This will be yet another experience for Tony and me, one that I am looking forward to very much.

Friday 15ᵗʰ June 2007

With all our business completed Tony and I got up this morning with Dima's birthday as the main focus. We are now staying in our own house in Veliko Tarnovo at 34, Gurko Street. We have breakfast there and sometimes lunch. We continue to eat out in the evenings, but the food is so good and the prices so low it is silly to do otherwise. Tony likes hotels whereas I get fed up with the constant need to engage with people, however nice they are. So I am really happy in our own space. Dima and Nicky have done such a great job preparing the place for occupation; the final touch was four bottles of Zagorka in the fridge. It really is a lovely little house.

Yesterday Nicky and Dima took us to see our newly renovated house in Tunel Street. As anticipated Nicky had done a fabulous job of the renovation. He is very knowledgeable about old Bulgarian architecture and has a real feel for how these old houses should look. As with Gurko Street he has fully modernised the house whilst maintaining the building's original charm.

We have bought some wine for Dima and later today we will pick up some flowers for her. However, we would like to get her a 'proper' present that requires a bit more imagination. We both know from trying to get things for our wives and family that shopping for presents in Bulgaria is a complete nightmare. There is simply so little on offer. Luckily Tony had what he thought was a brainwave. At the top of town is a little book shop selling mainly second hand British books. It is run by a delightfully eccentric English woman who moved to Veliko Tarnovo permanently a few years ago. She has told us on previous visits that the book shop is now her main form of income, although how good an income it produces I am not sure. Certainly in the three or four times I have visited the shop I have never seen another customer and I myself have only once made a purchase. "I am sure that the last time we went she had a book about Wales with lots of really nice pictures." said Tony with characteristic confidence. "We are always saying how beautiful Wales is and I think Dima would be interested to see some scenes and read about it." It was true that we often spoke of Tony's homeland and my adopted home and it was also true that Dima seemed interested in where we came from. "Do you think the book will still be there?" I ventured. "It was a year ago that we last visited her." "Who would have bought it?" said Tony. "Nobody but me would have even noticed it, and anyway she never has any customers!"

We decided to give it a try. The great thing about VT is that the town is really compact and you can get about easily on foot. In fact the streets in the old town are so narrow with the upper floor of many houses jutting out into the street it would be a real challenge to try and travel around in a car. We arrived at the bookshop after ten minutes. As usual, the English owner sat stooped over her laptop in the corner of the shop. Otherwise there was nobody there. After an exchange of greetings I started to tell the 'bookwoman' as we called her what we wanted. However, before I had completed my enquiry Tony stepped forward with the book in his hand. The book was a nineteen fifties hardback publication. It was in poor condition. All the photographs were black and white and some were quite faded. Just inside the front cover I made two discoveries. Firstly the original price of the book was 'one and six', about eight pence, and secondly it appeared to belong to Cheshire County Council Libraries. The bookwoman eulogised over the ancient tome and told us that it would be ours for just twelve leva, about five pounds. I thought the price was outrageous, but as far as Tony was concerned no price was too high for a book about his homeland.

Tony's afternoon was now defined for him. We returned to the house for a simple lunch. While I made a cheese on toast and put the kettle on for some tea Tony settled down on the couch to read the book that we had ostensibly bought for Dima. When the time came to collect the flowers Tony sent me off to fetch them with a dismissive wave of the hand. When I returned and suggested it was time to get ready he would not be dragged away from the book. When I complained that he now had ten minutes to get ready before we set off he reluctantly put the book aside. I feared that he was no longer prepared to give the book away, but I was mistaken. "She'll love that." he proclaimed and almost before I could tie my shoelaces he was ready to go.

This was the first time we had properly been inside Dima's and Nicky's house and it was a revelation. Like our little house in Gurko Street it backs onto the River Yantra and, as with our house, from the street it appears to be very small. It is in fact enormous. The main living room opens out towards the river and to get to it you descend several long staircases. Everything in the vast lounge seems suitable for a giant with the room dominated by a massive open fireplace. Despite the time of year Nicky was burning logs that were so huge they could normally not be lifted onto the fire by one man. Nicky, however, seemed able to accomplish this feat on his own without apparent difficulty. Various artefacts were to be found hanging on the walls, inserted into umbrella stands or sitting on tables. These artefacts included a vast collection of old weapons: rifles, hand guns, swords and bayonets. Nicky proudly showed his weapon collection to Tony apparently, as Dima explained later, omitting me from this honour on the grounds that I was a vegetarian.

The guests sat around a table that would not have seemed out of place in a castle and each of them greeted us warmly. We had feared that all the other guests would be in their late twenties and early thirties, but we were pleased to discover that that the friends, neighbours and family covered the full age range. Dima's parents took pride of place. It was becoming clear that the evening would be in essence a dinner party, another new experience for us and so we gratefully accepted a glass of beer together with a Rakia and started to relax, not difficult in the company of Dima and Nicky. Soon afterwards the first course, a variety of salads, arrived on the table. Instead of everyone taking up their cutlery and beginning their meal, our Bulgarian friends and their guests took the arrival of the salad as a sign to lean back in their chairs and light up a cigarette. Tony and I felt like thieves caught red-handed as we scooped salad onto our plates and then looked around to see that everyone else's plate was empty. We slowly and gently put our knives and forks back onto the table. About twenty minutes passed during which time an incredible number of cigarettes were smoked, but there was almost no activity regarding the food. A neighbour aged about fifty five had put a small amount of cucumber salad onto his plate and taken two or three forkfuls, but other than that nobody seemed interested.

As time passed Tony and I were fearing that nobody would ever eat anything and hunger was starting to get the better of us. Whilst continuing to chat with the other guests, we slowly but surely put fork to mouth and ate what was on our plate. Eventually one or two people put very small amounts of food onto their plates and ate at the speed of snails. Meanwhile Nicky had disappeared into the kitchen to finish off cooking the main course, ably assisted by his mother in law. More than an hour and a half after the first course had been put out Dima's mother came back to the table and, after an affirmative nod from her daughter and a glance around the guests, she started to clear away the salads, eighty per cent of which still remained.

Half an hour later the main course was brought out. This consisted of huge platefuls of fried pork with sauté potatoes. For me alone, as a non-meat eater there was a pile of fried fish that would have been easily enough for the whole ensemble. Now surely, the guests would set to, I felt sure, but as before the first reaction was to light up and sit back as if nobody had noticed that the food had been served. I remembered my brother–in-law Paul once telling me about a meal he had at the home of a teacher colleague during an exchange visit to Russia. He had told me that given the food shortages there the family had eaten almost nothing for a week so that they could serve up a proper feast when he came to dinner. He had then sat in front of his plate waiting for the host to give some sort of signal before eventually realising they were all waiting for him and only after he had eaten an ample amount did any of the family help themselves. I thought at first that something similar was going on and following Paul's experience I started to eat and Tony followed suit. However, after we had both cleared our plate, there was still no sign of any Bulgarians eating. Since this time I have witnessed the same behaviour in restaurants all over Bulgaria. I have asked Bulgarians what this is about and the only comment I have ever received is that they cannot understand how British people can eat food when it is so hot.

On this particularly evening I just ate what seemed a polite amount and as the beer and Rakia flowed I stopped worrying about it. I was at least reassured that no such timidity was being displayed with regard to the drinks. As the evening wore on the guests became louder and more high-spirited. They all showed a lot of interest in what Tony and I were doing and both Dima and Desi worked overtime translating and thereby ensuring that nobody was ever excluded from the conversation. A particular friendship seemed to be forming between Tony and the middle-aged neighbour who had earlier been the first to take a fork to his salad. With the help of Desi as an interpreter – she is brilliant at it – Tony and Ivan were exchanging stories and views about being patriots of small nations under the shadow of larger oppressive countries. I was not sure that I recognised a lot of what Tony described as the relationship between England and Wales, but he was astute enough to see that it was playing well to his audience and so continued. He and his new friend were enjoying themselves and given that, he was entitled to a little poetic license.

Suddenly the evening took an interesting new direction as Ivan, the neighbour gave a rendition of a Bulgarian folk song. I assume it was quite sentimental as the whole congregation listened with a serious expression on their faces and the singer fought, not always successfully, to hold back the tears. As soon as Ivan was finished Tony took up the challenge singing a Welsh folk song at full volume which was not only competently sung, but was also well acted as Tony, with arms and facial expressions, mimed out the song as he sang. The neighbour responded immediately and so it went on for a total of about ten songs. I knew that Tony's repertoire was almost used up when he sang a boring and repetitive song about an umbrella that was often sung by English kids attending Welsh schools as a fairly easy introduction to the Welsh language. Not wanting to see him outdone, I lead the guests in a prolonged applause that indicated to the two performers that their audience were satisfied. The two small nation compatriots hugged each other and became brothers for life. It was a great evening.

Saturday 16th June 2007

We had got to bed very late last night and Tony and I slept in, something we rarely did in Bulgaria because we were always so busy. We had only been out of bed for about half an hour when the phone rang and it was Dima asking us if we wanted to go for a day out. This was really nice, not only because we were at a loose end, but also because it told us that they were not yet fed up with our company.

The trip they had planned was to a museum village called Etar where all the crafts and the architecture of the Bulgarian National Revival period could be seen. This was just the sort of thing that interested both Tony and me and so we were ready to roll when Nicky and Dima pulled up outside our little house in the old Mercedes about half an hour later. Etar was just beyond the town of Gabrovo, a journey of around thirty five miles. In normal circumstances it would have taken us about fifty minutes, but that was not taking account of the need to continuously stop and fill the Mercedes up with water. At first we were stopping every fifteen minutes, but as the radiator got warmer the Mercedes' thirst grew and by the time we arrived at Etar it was every two minutes. Nicky was completely unfazed by the whole thing and Dima told us in a completely matter of fact way that this condition had been worsening over a period of twelve months, but so far Nicky had not got round to having it fixed.

The historical village of Etar was remarkable. The architecture was all from the Renaissance period and in each house there was a workshop in which some old craft or trade was being carried out. Museums presented in this way are so much more enjoyable than simple exhibits. Tony and I were fascinated and Nicky and Dima were glad that their idea for a day out had been so well judged. The weather was absolutely beautiful and at the end of the village street was an open air restaurant where we were more than glad to stand our special friends a meal. So perfect was the day that the return journey with the constant filling of the radiator just struck us as funny. Tony and I were now firmly in love with this part of Bulgaria and from now on all our trips would include a bus journey to Veliko Tarnovo.

2014: Getting Things Done: The Bulgarian Way

Monday 5th May 2014

The last time I was in Bulgaria I had with Nicky's help bought a car, an old Nissan Primera. Now that I was here and using it, I needed to register the vehicle in my name. At home that involves completing a small slip on the registration document and sending it to the Driver and Vehicle Licensing Authority (DVLA). A week or so later a new registration document arrives in the post and that's it. Not so in Bulgaria. Here it involves physically taking the vehicle to the traffic police where a long and bureaucratic process takes place. This includes a technical inspection (the Bulgarian equivalent of an MOT) even if the last such inspection had been carried out just a month ago. It gets worse. Nicky and Dima, who were going to undertake this task with me, informed me that because I had bought the car through my company and the company was registered in Varna then that is where we had to go to register the car.

Nicky had some experience in these matters and knew that there was only one centre for this process in Varna and that every day they were over-run. Nevertheless when he told me to be at his house at three in the morning I thought it a bit excessive. How wrong can you be? When we arrived at the traffic police authority in Varna at five thirty there was already a queue of cars more than a hundred metres long. We joined the queue and proceeded to do what British people hate and Bulgarians seem not to mind, i.e. to wait…..and wait…..and wait. There was much speculation amongst the waiting customers about when the centre would actually open. I suggested to Nicky and Dima that they were sure to open early, given the numbers waiting. Nicky gave me an indulgent smile that seemed to say, "Poor naïve fool!" He was right to be sceptical: the office opened at half past nine by which time there was a line of cars stretching out of sight. It was already clear that those cars who were still joining the queue would not be seen at all that day.

Once the office was opened the first twenty or so car owners were invited to submit their documents to the office to be checked. Sadly we were not amongst this first elite group. After the documents had been checked the owners were told, not in order, to drive their car through the gates, which were patrolled by four police officers, into the yard. They then disappeared from sight and although some came out thirty minutes later brandishing new number plates others remained inside for hours. As I had very little idea what the criteria were for successful registration I started to get anxious regarding whether this monumental undertaking would end in failure. Nicky told me not to worry and that it would be fine, although I could see no evidence for his confident assertion. Nicky was firmly of the belief that the purpose of the exercise was to put you through the wringer, but that in the end your car would be registered.

I still feared the possibility of having to come back for some reason and the part of the process that I most worried about was the technical inspection. At home, except on the odd occasions when I have owned fairly new cars, I have never submitted a vehicle for an MOT without having it checked and if necessary the faults rectified first. I honestly had no idea about the condition of my car, beyond the obvious. However, looking around me at some of the other cars being submitted for inspection did provide some degree of reassurance. There were some old Ladas and some even older Russian models that seemed to be held together by rust and bits of twine.

Amongst those queueing in front of me was a small lorry with an ancient Trabant – the famous model from East Germany – loaded on top. As the lorry got nearer the front of the queue, the driver tried to prevent the vehicles behind him closing the gap created as he pulled forward. This caused great consternation and several arguments broke out as a result. Eventually his reasons became clear. When he had finally established a small runway behind him he put some old metal ramps down and suddenly the old Trabant was rolled off the back and bump started as it landed on terra firma. The engine burst into life accompanied by a plume of black smoke. The 'Trabi' was ready for inspection.

At two o clock, after the office had been closed an hour for lunch we finally reached the point where we were invited to submit our documents. They must have been in good order because ten minutes later we were asked to drive the Nissan into the yard. All three of us got into the car with Nicky at the wheel, but as we approached the gate one of the police officers stopped us abruptly and informed us that only the driver was allowed through. Dima attempted to explain that I was the owner, but they were helping me because I neither understood the process (did anybody?) nor spoke Bulgarian. She might as well have saved her breath. One person could go through with the car and Nicky was the only choice. So with Dima and me repelled Nicky ventured forward alone and the gate was closed in front of the legitimate owner's face. Nicky and the Nissan soon disappeared from sight.

Nicky had been gone for more than an hour when Dima's phone rang. The delay had not been due to the condition of the car which was apparently quite acceptable. They had wanted to check the engine number against that in our documents and it was so covered in oil and muck that they could not read it. Nicky had been at work with a damp cloth and some detergent trying to clean the part of the engine where the number was stamped to make it legible. This had now been accomplished and the new documents were ready to be signed so I was needed as it was to be registered in the name of my company. Dima and I approached the barrier and before she had a chance to explain the same police officer barked at us to clear off. Dima stood her ground and patiently explained that the inspectors inside required my attendance. The policeman shouted at her even louder for good measure, but at the same time he sullenly raised the barrier.

At just before four in the afternoon we emerged triumphant with the car newly registered. It had only taken ten and a half hours.

Wednesday 7th May 2014

Today was a big day in the civic pride of Gabrovo, our nearest town. For two years the town's workforce has been working to repair the two kilometre long road that runs off from the main road down to the two large supermarkets, Billa and Kaufland. On each of our frequent trips here during that time we have been eager witnesses to the work's progress. It was for many years the worst road in the town, full of potholes and other more serious hazards. In places the road had sunk completely and along the length of the road the edges had all crumbled away. The dangers involved in driving to the supermarket of your choice were increased by the fact that in order to avoid holes cars frequently lurched at top speed onto the wrong side of the road and unexpectedly came speeding towards you. During the two years that it has taken to repair it the road had never until recently been closed. At first the many hazards that were created by the work itself were indicated by official road signs warning you of dangers ahead. As work progressed, albeit at a snail's pace, the town's store of road signs was obviously used up and hazards such as an uncovered manhole were brought to the attention of the driver by, for example, a branch ripped from a nearby tree sticking up out of the hole.

During the whole period of repair a machine was rarely seen, all the work apparently being undertaken by pure manpower. It was also notable that the application of this manpower was sporadic and intermittent. Sometimes it seemed no more than a handful of men could be spared for this work, whilst at other times it appeared that the whole workforce of the Municipality of Gabrovo was deployed there. However, on these latter occasions no more than ten per cent of the men, clad in yellow work suits and yellow wellies, seemed to be engaged at any one time while their workmates sat or slept on the grass banks nearby. It was easy to judge when a work surge was imminent as the men in yellow could suddenly be seen at every bus stop and lay-by around the town and nearby villages waiting for a bus or a lift.

When we arrived here at the beginning of April the road was at its most dangerous so far. Although the road surface was now good it was still six inches lower than the manhole covers which protruded dangerously without any warning signs, those having apparently been deployed elsewhere. In normal weather this was not too much of a problem as they were so prominent as to be clearly seen. However, a consistent characteristic of all drains in Bulgaria is that they have no capacity to receive water. Therefore after heavy rain the manholes were no longer visible and many a driver could be seen standing by his vehicle, up to his ankles in water staring helplessly at a burst tyre.

And then last week there were signs that the end could be in sight. Firstly, parts of the road were shut off for periods of time and secondly, as well as men in yellow there were yellow machines in action. The arrangements that were put in place when part of the road was closed were singular to say the least. There were no signs saying "Road closed ahead" and no diversion signs. Instead one was suddenly confronted by a road block in front of which a man in yellow sat comfortably on a dining room chair. Your options were then as follows: You could do a U-turn and find another way of your own choosing to your destination. This option seemed the most popular. Secondly, you could park up in the vain hope that the man in yellow would indicate what you should now do. This hope would however never be fulfilled and those that took this option soon realised it was in vain and turned back. The third option was to get out of the car and either foolishly remonstrate with the man in the chair or, more sensibly, negotiate a way forward with him. I was surprised to witness a few occasions when negotiations were successful and the man rose from his chair and opened the road for the car to pass. I never had insight into how this was managed, but I marvelled at the process.

Finally today every workman who had ever spent time on the road works seemed to be in attendance, their yellow clothing washed and pressed for the occasion. The last sentry attending the last road block rose from his seat, removing himself and his chair whilst his proud colleagues removed the barriers. In a completely proletariat ceremony with no town dignitaries present the "Road to Billa" was open.

Wednesday 28ᵗʰ May 2014

Last night we experienced a thunder storm like neither of us had ever witnessed before in our entire lives. At five thirty we were sitting on the balcony chatting and enjoying an early evening drink.

The horses were in the paddock just opposite and we had decided to leave them out for the night. The sun was shining and it was about twenty five degrees. We were feeling very relaxed and looking forward to sitting outside until bedtime as we had done the previous three evenings. Suddenly it started to get quite dark and we looked up to see a massive black cloud approaching. Within a few minutes a significant breeze started up and we knew that a thunder storm was on its way. As we launched ourselves into action this was confirmed by an almighty flash and a loud rumble almost immediately afterwards indicating the storm was nearby. We rushed across to get the horses, brought them into the stables on the yard and as we were heading for the house the heavens opened. Expecting torrential rain we found ourselves instead under siege from hailstones the size of golf balls. As they hit you it really hurt and we ran like mad to get inside the house. I have no idea how ice can fall out of the sky when just minutes before it was twenty five degrees, but then I did fail O level Geography. However it was possible within minutes the whole yard was covered in a thick layer of ice and it was still coming down.

The horses looked out over their stable doors with an expression of disbelief mixed with relief. Like me they were probably hoping the new roof built by the Lost Boys would hold up under the deluge. Thank goodness it did. By now the water coming off the downspouts from the gutters on the house was like a rapid waterfall. As an insurance against our pump or well failing during the summer months we had just acquired a one thousand litre water tank which we hoped to fill with water from the roof. We had earlier that day been bemoaning the fact that we had probably acquired the tank too late, just as the rainy season was coming to an end. We feared we would struggle to fill it. We now watched from the window as it filled before our eyes and after an hour and a half it was overflowing with water gushing across the yard.

The storm raged on and this morning we were faced with a scene of utter devastation. We have a vine growing across a trellis that acts as a roof for the area where we usually have breakfast. This vine had been doing so well, but now it hung limp and sad, almost devoid of leaves. All the bedding plants we had bought and recently planted were battered and pressed to the ground. Our fruit trees in the yard, cherry, apple and plum, had lost most of their young fruit and half of their leaves. The whole yard was full of the debris. This was upsetting, but was of little consequence when compared to the loss encountered by our neighbours.

As I have said previously they are very competent gardeners and this terrible storm and its devastating consequences hit them hard. If a keen vegetable grower in the UK had an equivalent loss they would be very downcast, but they would still have a choice of several supermarkets to fall back on for their veg and would probably visit a garden centre to buy plants of similar maturity to the ones they had lost, but it means so much more here because what they have in their garden is what they eat the whole year round. They eat what is seasonal and when the growing season is over and all crops have been harvested they eat what they have preserved earlier in the year. What they have very little of is cash and so replacing or buying in what they have lost is not so easy.

This morning everybody was on the street discussing the storm and so despite my limited grasp of their language I went to join the throng and to empathise with my neighbours. For the first time in my experience, Honeyman wore a sad expression. I had personally watched him and his father planting masses of tomato plants that he had cultivated from seed. In a combination of Bulgarian and German that he was sure to understand I asked if he had lost them all. "Domati kaput?" I enquired. His answer was devastating. "Sto protsenta." (One hundred percent). All the other neighbours looked on glumly as Honeyman went on to list his losses. It was too much to bear.

Most of our neighbours are very poor compared to almost anybody at home, but what they do have is fortitude. The next time I saw Honeyman, about two hours later he was entering his gate carrying a tray of about six tomato plants. His loss had been ten times this. Nevertheless he turned to me with a broad grin and the familiar twinkle in his eye. "Rezervi" he quipped and went into the garden to recommence planting.

That evening Honeyman's dad came shuffling into the yard with a plate bearing recently picked strawberries and a beautiful slice of honeycomb. The message was clear: we are down, but not out.

Monday 3rd June 2014

Today Nicky and Dima were visiting us when Nicky received a phone call from our security man. The house was alarmed and overseen by a security firm from Dryanovo. We had with Nicky's help put these arrangements in place because we had until now only used the place as a holiday home and so it had been empty most of the time. Given that we had the horses with us and most of the fields were not attached to the house we had recently decided that we would keep this arrangement in place. Although we did not particularly buy into the Bulgarian view that there was a strong likelihood of somebody attempting to steal the horses, we had come a long way with them and there was no sense in taking a chance now. The cost in any event was hardly prohibitive. The monthly payment was now due and up until now Nicky had been paying this on our behalf. Nicky informed the security guard that we were now living here and suggested he call at the house to collect our payment and also to meet us. This was absolutely necessary anyway because if the alarm went off and he came rushing over we would not want to be mistaken for villains. I had a feeling that his policy was act first and ask questions later.

About fifteen minutes later a huge guy dressed in black with a shaven head arrived. He had a hand gun stuck nonchalantly in the front of his trousers and his right hand was heavily bandaged. He shook hands, deploying his left hand and introduced himself as Nikolai. He noticed Marieluise looking at his injured hand and answered her unspoken question. "In Dryanovo – a little bit of trouble," he confided. "OK now!" We tried not to look alarmed and offered him a coffee. He declined, but sat down with us and chatted for a bit using Dima as an interpreter. We told him about the horses and he at once asked to see them. Guinness and Flo were at that moment in the stables so it was easy to introduce Nikolai to them. He was remarkably gentle with them and both horses seemed to like him.

Nikolai then sat back down and handed us a business card with his mobile number on it. He made a sign to indicate the making of a phone call and explained that we merely needed to say: "Todorcheta – panic" and he would be there in seven minutes. He was very precise about the time. I paid him two months money to save him calling so often. He thanked me, went over to the horses again to say goodbye and with a polite nod of the head he was gone. If Marieluise had ever been worried about her own security and that of her horses she wasn't worried now. Nikolai was the man.

2008: Decision Time; Cashing In

Tuesday 17th June 2008

These days our flights to Bulgaria were easy and cheap. Budget airlines had discovered Bulgaria and Bulgarians, now members of the European Union, had discovered Britain. In spite of the outrageous laws imposed to make them second class EU members with restrictions on their travel, significant numbers were finding their way to all parts of the UK.

Today we were arriving in Sofia with a busy schedule ahead of us. During the early part of the year we had been watching the housing market in Bulgaria and had eventually decided that now was the time to sell. We were very aware that the housing boom here and the subsequent rise in the value of property had been largely fuelled by the British friendly invasion. It could and would not last forever and although the market was still on the up we were sure that now was the time. We did not want to be greedy and risk a downturn. We had been in touch with Georgi from Address in Varna and also with Rada. Rada, as our solicitor rightly remained neutral on the subject of whether to sell, but Georgi was firmly in agreement with our decision. He was confident that he would be able to sell the three apartments at a good profit.

There was another consideration. When we had bought the properties the pound had been strong and was worth about 1.45 Euros. Now the Euro was strong, the rate was now at about 1.10, so if we sold in Euros and converted it to pounds we would make a good profit even without the increase in the value of the properties.

But for now we were heading for Veliko Tarnovo. Primarily we needed to get the apartments on the market and so most of our business was in Varna. However, we also intended to speak with Desi about whether to put the houses in Veliko Tarnovo on the market. For now though we were simply breaking our journey to Varna. Six hours on a bus, the time it would take to go directly from Sofia to Varna was not something we were prepared to undertake. We got off the bus at VT and as was now our custom headed for the Humphrey Bogart bar.

After a few pints there we set off to our little house in Gurko Street. As we got to the start of the street I noticed that the little shop at the entrance to Gurko Street was now an estate agency, Classic Bulgaria. The name sounded familiar and suddenly I remembered that this was the agency that had been opened by the beautiful Kremena, the former Address agency representative that had sold 34, Gurko Street to me. Curiosity got the better of me and we entered the tiny office. Kremena was not there, but her equally beautiful sister was there to take messages until her return later that evening. We said our names and made it clear it was no more than a social call, but when the sister asked us to leave our number it seemed impolite not to give it.

Ten minutes later, just as we were putting our bags down at the house, the lovely Kremena rang. Whizzing through the formalities Kremena got quickly to the point of the call. She had a house for sale in Gurko Street that she was sure would suit us. We explained to her that we were now selling rather than buying, but she remained adamant that it was worth us looking at it. She said she had remembered that we particularly liked Gurko Street and that this house was twice the size of the one we currently owned. As with her sister earlier politeness got the better of us and we agreed to meet her at her office in fifteen minutes.

I have absolutely no idea why the lovely Kremena wanted to show us this house. When the three of us arrived at the house there was a reception committee from the family to meet us. We had come to regard this as normal as we had experienced it many times in VT and in Varna. The family's nominated spokesperson proceeded to show us around the house extoling its virtues as we went. Tony and I had no intention of buying the house, but tried to show a polite level of interest indicating we were taking it seriously without getting their hopes up. After all, we did not want to use up time that could otherwise be spent in the Cave drinking Zagorka.

We went fairly quickly from room to room until we came to the last room in the house that was mysteriously locked. We stood aside expecting someone to open up, but the family acted as if the room was not there. "What about this room?" Tony enquired, interested for the first time. "Very nice room. This very nice room" was the answer from the appointed spokesperson. "Well let's see it then" Tony persisted. "This room locked today. Maybe next time." Now I too was intrigued. "We would really not want to come back to see one room." I suggested, but this room was staying shut. We started to lose interest, after all we were not going to buy the house even if the locked room housed the Bulgarian equivalent of the Crown Jewels. We headed for the exit and as we got outside we both turned to look at the exterior of the house. Immediately our eyes were drawn to the roof. The part of the roof above the 'very nice room' was completely collapsed with the roof timbers and the tiles having fallen inside the building. We both gave the lovely Kremena a hard stare. Although it is difficult to look sternly at someone who looks like an angel, I think we both managed it quite well, because she visibly wilted under our gaze. We did not need to confirm that we would not be putting in an offer on the house. However, Kremena did not remain down for long and before we left she managed to tell us that she could manage the sale of our existing houses on a lower commission than we were currently paying. This time we explicitly confirmed that we would not be taking up her offer.

Within a very short time we were sitting having a drink with Nicky and Dima in their new local, our equilibrium restored. Reluctantly they had been forced on a point of principle to forsake the Cave, their previous haunt which Tony and I loved. One evening they had been sitting at one of the three outside tables having a beer. They were at this time one of the bar's best customers. An English family came in for a meal and although there was no outside table free they told the landlord that they preferred to sit outside. The landlord instead of telling them that they would have to wait until a table became free asked Nicky and Dima to move inside. That was the last time the landlord ever saw them.

Wednesday 18th June 2008

At about eleven in the morning we caught a bus to Varna. By four in the afternoon we had booked into a hotel in the city centre and were sitting with Georgi in the Address office. We confirmed our plans to sell all three apartments and agreed the prices with Georgi who was confident he could get somewhere near the asking price on each property. Georgi then invited Ivo to join us and the two of them conferred over whether we should give notice to the tenants given our desire to sell up. Ivo advised us that one of the tenants was planning to move out soon anyway and there was clearly no point looking for another. Regarding the other tenancies, both Ivo and Georgi felt that there was no need to give notice as there were rarely problems getting tenants to move out. Remembering the poor woman in Veliko Tarnovo who was the tenant of 34, Gurko Street I felt sure they were correct. We then paid a visit to Rada, who as usual seemed pleased to see us, and updated her. As always there was some bureaucratic business to see to, but as Rada had prepared the ground it did not take too long.

And that was in essence our business in Varna completed. After going to the bank to check our balance we were free for the rest of the evening. We decided that we should on this occasion have an evening out in the city centre that we had many times planned to do but never done due to our allegiances to the Fox in Varna. We went back to the hotel for a shower and then headed for town. After visiting three highly recommended city bars we realised that our hearts just weren't in it. At home in North Wales Tony and I almost never drink anywhere but the Fox in our own parish. We are creatures of habit and there was no point fighting it. Soon we were receiving a heroes' welcome in the Fox in Varna and there we stayed until his stock of Zagorka ran aground. We returned to the hotel happy. Tomorrow we would be returning to VT.

Friday 20th June 2008

Back in Veliko Tarnovo we called at Address to see Desi and her boss. It had always been our practice to do all our business first and today was no exception. As in the past our experiences dealing with Address in Veliko Tarnovo were in direct contrast to how things were with their colleagues in Varna. Whereas Georgi had given us really clear guidance on price we could not get the same explicit advice from Desi and her manager. Maybe it is because the market is so much slower here than in Varna and so they have less to base it on. Also the houses in Veliko Tarnovo are all so unique in themselves it is perhaps harder to set prices. Whatever the reason Tony and I had to take the lead on this and in the end we decided on a value for each house with no clear idea of how realistic we were being. That evening we had a drink with Desi, Dima and Nicky, but even after a few beers Desi was still saying "It is up to you."

Tuesday 24th June 2008

As we arrived home we were aware that we were entering a new phase with regard to our business in Bulgaria. We were both excited and apprehensive about what would happen next. Would we get quick sales or would it drag on for years? We hoped that the prices were about right and would generate some interest. On the other hand if our houses and apartments did sell would this mean the end of our big adventure?

Wednesday 17th December 2008

At the end of November Georgi had been in touch to say that he had a buyer for one of the large apartments and just ten days ago he was in touch again to say that someone had put a holding deposit on the second one. Rada had dealt with the preliminary contracts and had weaved her magic so that we could complete on the two properties at the same time. When we had given Rada power of attorney to act on our behalf she had advised that she should be allowed to complete purchases on our behalf as that was what we needed at the time, but not sales. This was Rada acting with propriety which was proper, but as far as we were concerned not necessary. However, at the time we were not thinking of selling and had let it go so this is how things now stood. Given it was nearly Christmas and we both had family things to see to we were, for the first time ever, not particularly enamoured with the idea of a trip to Bulgaria. Nevertheless, we knew how important this was. If these sales came off we would be able to give every member of the group the whole of their original investment back on the sale of just two properties. This was important to us as it put to bed any anxiety over the whole thing being a flop. So after griping about it we went ahead and booked a flight to Sofia. We had now arrived in Varna after a six hour bus journey fit for little else than finding the hotel and going to bed.

However, as a representative of Great Britain one has certain obligations when abroad and it would have been churlish not to have visited our old haunt, the Fox in Varna. It was only ten minutes' walk and although we were very tired the thought of a few pints at our Varna local revived us considerably. It is interesting to note that in Britain landlords come and go and bar and kitchen staff rotate even more frequently. This even applies to our own local in North Wales where the pub always has the same regulars, but the landlords only stay for two or three years. This ever repeating pattern often caused Tony to say, "It's our pub, they are just passing through." In Bulgaria, on the other hand, you can go to the same bar or restaurant over a period of years and find the same owner and same staff each time. So it was at the Fox in Varna and we entered to see the same old faces on both sides of the bar and the same cook hovering in the background hoping for an order. However, by this time we were beyond hunger and just concentrated on the beer. The landlord had obviously not been expecting us and it was too late in the evening for him to send out for fresh supplies, so as a result it did not take long for us to see off his stock of Zagorka. This suited us fine as we really needed to get to bed, not only because we were tired, but also because we had two property completions to attend the following day and we needed to be reasonably sharp.

Thursday 18th December 2008

The first completion went off without a hitch. The second completion took place at the same notary with the sale going to a

Bulgarian woman. She had told Rada beforehand that she had not had time to organise a bank transfer and she felt nervous about carrying a large sum of money around. She and Rada had agreed that we would complete the formalities at the Notary's office and we would then all accompany her to her bank where she would make a withdrawal and pay us the huge sum in cash. After we had done the deal we all got up to leave the notary's office. I must admit I have never in all my dealings in Bulgaria felt so nervous. In law the apartment now belonged to the Bulgarian woman, but she still owed us over one hundred thousand pounds. What would we have been able to do if she had simply said "Thanks very much" and walked away, or more likely disputed the amount she still owed us? In the taxi to the bank I expressed this anxiety to Rada, but her simple answer was that it would not happen. Thank heavens she was as usual correct. After the two property deals Tony and I left the bank carrying the largest sum of money either of us had ever seen let alone handled. For now we did not even want to think about the next problem, how to get the money home.

Saturday 20th December 2008

We arrived home mid-afternoon in time for the start of Christmas. Mine started with a bang as the whole family had tickets to see the Rock n Roll pantomime at Theatr Clwyd that evening. For some years now this had been the Hart family's official start to Yuletide. As usual the panto did not disappoint and later that evening as I sat with Marieluise, Lucy, Emily and their blokes consuming the buffet that Marieluise had spent half the day preparing, I felt at ease with the world. A family Christmas had begun and this was my favourite time of year, but there was a big added bonus. Four and a half years ago Tony and I had almost unwittingly persuaded many of our friends and neighbours to part with a quarter of a million pounds of hard earned money for us to invest in Bulgaria as we saw fit. It was a great act of trust from them and, although Tony told the group again and again that they should not invest their money unless they could afford to lose it, we felt a heavy responsibility. Now with just two properties sold we could start the New Year by returning the whole of their investment. During this four year period Tony and I had heard many stories of people making bad investments in Bulgaria and sometimes losing large sums of money. We had often discussed over a beer opening a company to help people recoup their losses from property dealing in Bulgaria, "IfouledupinBulgaria.com". The idea was not entirely frivolous. As I sat there with a pint in one hand and an egg sarnie in the other I realised that what we had achieved at this point was not only a relief to me and to Tony it was also one hell of an achievement.

2009: New Life; Sad Endings

Monday 11th May 2009

We had booked our flight some time ago; obviously we did not know at that point that we would arrive in Veliko Tarnovo just days after Dima gave birth to a beautiful little girl who Nicky and Dima named Neda. We felt both privileged and slightly awkward having arrived at the time of such a personal event. Dima and Nicky, however, seemed glad that we were there to meet little Neda and showed her off proudly to us.

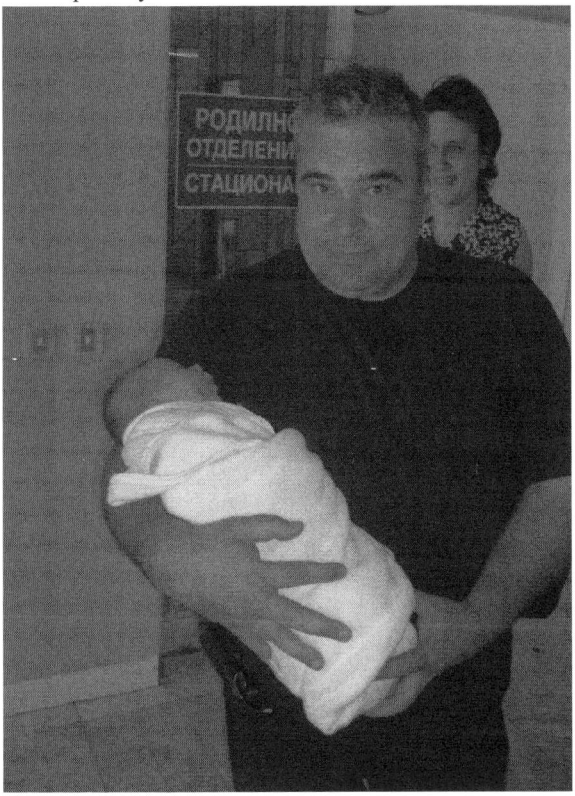

The proud father holding his daughter Neda

Neda was, and still is, a beautiful little girl and both parents were infatuated with her. It was great to see them so happy. Despite having her hands full – literally – Dima had managed to get 34 Gurko Street ready for us and after visiting the new arrival we settled into our little Bulgarian home. We had already been to Varna and reviewed the selling price of the small apartment with Georgi and now we intended to meet up with Desi to review the sale prices of the two renovated houses in Veliko Tarnovo. With everyone having now received their stake back we were not in a hurry to sell, although we were aware that the housing market across Europe was starting to come under pressure. Our friends back home were certainly not pressurising us for a quick sale and on the whole we felt we were in this for the long haul.

It was great to see Desi again and as usual she made us laugh, redefining her friend Dima's finest hour as just more time without being able to drink. Her advice to us regarding the houses was simple: There was not much going on in the market and a price reduction would probably make little difference to the saleability of the two houses, so just sit tight. We agreed with that and as it was now early evening we adjourned to the pub, Desi wanting to emphasise that she had no intention of abstaining as an act of solidarity with her best mate. So with fortitude we set about wetting the baby's head. We took our duties seriously and stuck to the task doggedly until doubt as to whether we could manage to walk home forced us to conclude a very pleasant day and evening.

On that beautiful May evening sitting outside one of our favourite bars in Veliko Tarnovo all the things we loved about Bulgaria and the times we had enjoyed there seemed to be crystallised. We had made some great friends, especially Dima and Nicky and had been lucky enough to share in the birth of their daughter. Our property investment, after all this was what brought us here, had gone well. Whether as a continuation of our property business or just to visit friends we were sure that we would be coming back here for many years to come. We could never have imagined what fate held in store for Tony and that in just a few months everything would change.

Tuesday 8th December 2009

On 27th September Tony had reached the age of sixty. He was never one to over celebrate birthdays, but this one was particularly muted as he had been unwell for some time. I called at his house to give him a present. I can recall that it was a golf book and I think it was fairly light-hearted, but I am not honestly sure. I could see he was not well, but he was giving little away. He was trying to make light of his situation - I thought he could succeed in making light of anything – but it was not working. In some indefinable way the Tony I knew and loved was not there in that room. I went away feeling concerned, but unclear as to what was going on. Not long afterwards I knew. He told me so bravely that he had liver cancer and the prognosis was poor, actually worse than poor. He finished his news with "Well, there you are. Now that I have spoken to you, everyone who needs to know, has been told. I'll fight it, of course I will, but... well you know."

It was one of the worse moments of my life, but today I was trying vainly to be upbeat. Tony's wife Kay had asked me to speak at his funeral and I had no intention of letting her down. Most of all I was not going to let him down. Despite how I was feeling I was going to make people laugh. It was of course what he would have wanted. Dima had once said to me that she thought Tony had been put on this world to make people happy. I was determined to keep this in mind even at his passing.

I was sitting near the front of the church with my wife and daughters all of whom were silently sobbing. I tried to cut them off from me. Kay had also asked if I wanted to be a pallbearer, but I knew that if I carried out that sombre undertaking I would never be able to complete the main task so soon afterwards. As the coffin was carried into the church I looked away and repeated under my breath the parts of my speech that I knew would most likely trip me up. I had been doing this all week, out loud as I drove the car or when alone in the house. I figured that if I said the most difficult words often enough I would be able to just run through them on the day. The vicar called me up and I was by now surprisingly composed. The church was packed like it has never been before or since. There were many more people waiting respectfully outside as not an extra soul could have been wedged into the beautiful old church. My ploy worked and I was able to make my dedication and give my condolences to his lovely family without breaking up.

Before I knew it I was into anecdotes about him. All through my career I had done a lot of public speaking and I fell back on the well-used tactic of looking at just one person. I chose Alan Bridson, another of Tony's closest friends. I looked at him because I knew that despite his sadness he would be eager to laugh. As I told some of the amusing, often hilarious stories about Tony I felt the weight of the task falling away. I included many stories about our experiences together in Bulgaria. He had once told me that it had been his biggest adventure so it was fitting. With Kay's prior permission I had included the story about Tony telling Rada that it was a Welsh custom to kiss your solicitor. It got the biggest laugh. Somehow, the audacity of it summed him up. It had been our greatest adventure, but from now on it was mine alone.

2010: Four Pilgrims Venture Forth

Tuesday 30ᵗʰ March 2010

After Tony's death Kay and I had been diligent in sorting out the formal ownership of the Bulgarian company. The position of the shareholders was regulated by agreements made at home, whereas 'Bulgaria Property Mutual' as the company in Bulgaria was called had belonged to Tony and me. Tony's will had been straightforward in that he left everything to Kay and so this was the basis that Rada worked from. First of all she had needed everything, death certificate, will etc., to be authenticated by a British notary. I had never come across a notary at home. Although they are central to most contractual arrangements in the rest of Europe that is not the case in Britain. However I did find one tucked away in a law firm in Liverpool. Unfortunately his relative rarity was reflected in his fees. I took an oath never to complain about notary fees in Bulgaria again. So with the ownership of the company now sorted I needed someone to accompany me to Bulgaria to meet everyone and to know the ropes. This would be important in case there was urgent business to attend to for which I was not available. Tony and I had discussed this before he died and his son Sion had been nominated.

Sion and I were now on our way to Bulgaria, accompanied by mine and Tony's close friend Richard and my youngest daughter, Lucy. They had rather dubiously put themselves forward as first and second reserve to Sion, but in reality they were just along for the ride. As far as I was concerned this was great. It was potentially going to be a difficult trip for me and having Lucy as support and Rich as someone capable of lightening the mood was very welcome. On the EasyJet flight from Manchester to Sofia I sat next to Lucy who rather like her mother fell asleep ten minutes out. I therefore read my book most of the way and after we had entered the airport I realised that, not for the first time, I had left my reading glasses in the basket on the plane. Because I make a habit of this I had at least brought a spare pair.

It was strange for me making this familiar journey with three people for whom it was completely unfamiliar. Richard had been to Golden Sands with his wife Dawn, but Sion and Lucy had never set foot in Bulgaria. I felt the absence of Tony acutely and also felt oddly responsible for my fellow travellers. I had worked out an itinerary for the trip which made it easier for me, but I was still nervous and terribly on edge. This showed itself when we stepped outside the bus station to find our bus to Veliko Tarnovo. Looking right instead of left I almost walked under the wheels of a massive single decker powering out of the coach park. Lucy stopped me just in time and from that point on seemed to realise that I was not myself and took on the role of minder.

Richard wanted to sit next to me on the bus and leave the two youngsters to sit together, but Lucy, fearing some further mishap, insisted on sitting with her dad. This did not work out well for Sion. Before boarding the bus Richard had studied its roadworthiness using all his knowledge and experience as a wagon driver and plant hire owner. I don't think he was impressed and spent most of the journey regaling Sion with all the mechanical faults that he had noted and the terrible consequences that could follow. Sion, usually a self-confident young man, left the bus a gibbering wreck. Luckily I had just the antidote and on arrival in Veliko Tarnovo I led the party to the Humphrey Bogart bar where in the beautiful warm sunshine they sampled their first Zagorka.

I had told Dima that we would meet her at 34, Gurko Street directly from the bus so after enjoying our first pint I suggested to my reluctant fellow travellers that we should ring Dima and go to the house. Sion, following closely in his father's footsteps, wanted another Zagorka. When I objected he called for a vote and immediately three hands went up in support of his motion. I sat with my mouth open as my disloyal daughter called the barmaid across and ordered four more beers. As far as I was aware she only drank cider, but she had obviously adopted the sentiments of the motto, 'when in Rome'. Her Zagorka was sliding down as quickly as everybody else's. When the second pint had been dispatched I stood to leave, but the other three remained seated and again as Sion called for a vote three hands were raised in support of staying. I tried everything to get them to go, even suggesting that we had business to conduct and it was not fair to the group of investors to sit about getting pissed. "Forget the group, have another Zagorka." suggested Sion, again eerily redolent of his father. I have no idea how many times the vote was repeated, but by the time we set off to meet Dima a combination of anxiety, nervous exhaustion and drinking each pint too quickly had taken its toll on me and I was decidedly the worst for wear.

Finally we got to Gurko Street to meet Dima and after a quick tour of the house we went with her to meet Nicky at their local bar. I should have had one more and then called it a day, but instead I continued to drink. I had not eaten and after about an hour it suddenly struck me that I was going to do something daft if I did not get myself home. "That's it. I've had it!" I said suddenly and was already walking away before Dima and Nicky realised what was going on. The other three caught on quick and I stumbled off down the hill, with my entourage watching over me. I had left my Bulgarian friends without a proper farewell and for this I later got a telling off from both Lucy and Richard. Tomorrow we were off to Varna, but at least I would be back in a few days to make my peace.

Wednesday 31st March 2010

Today we arrived in Varna where the plan was to meet Rada and Georgi. Obviously Rada would be involved in any future business and Georgi was significant as he would be handling any potential sale of the small apartment. The visits were designed to allow Sion and our two Bulgarian partners to get acquainted. In all other respects they were no more than social calls. This was nice for me as I had got to like both of them a great deal over the years. I think they were pleased to see me too and also welcomed the opportunity to give their condolences regarding Tony face to face with a member of his family. For my daughter Lucy, as a young female solicitor herself, it was particularly interesting to meet Rada and they got on really well. Sion and Richard for their part were content just to look at her.

The visits done we were free to look around Varna and all three of them liked the city. They were particularly taken with the cathedral which is very impressive indeed and were quite perturbed to discover that the area around this holy place was dominated by money lenders and unsavoury characters trying to do money exchange deals. They were all intrigued by the physical appearance of the different generations of Varna people. The young people are generally good looking, slim and straight, and dressed similarly to youngsters from the big cities all over Europe. The older generation on the other hand bear the hallmarks of hard physical work and poor diet. They are commonly overweight and often quite bent. The older generation of women universally favour red tinted hair, often worn in a bird's nest style. Richie insisted that the older men all had square heads although I think the evidence for this is quite patchy. Sion liked this idea and speculated that their heads must have been put in a clamp when very young rather like the old practice of binding girls' feet in Japan to ensure their feet remained small and dainty. Later on in the day as the beer flowed these ideas were given more credence until we were all convinced about Sion's head clamp theory which he now suggested could be attached to people's heads as they slept.

It was inevitable that at some point in the evening Sion and Lucy would want to visit the Fox in Varna and sure enough about half way through the evening they asked me if we could go there. At first I agreed but when we reached the place I found myself unable to enter. The pain of going in without Tony and then on top of that having to explain his absence was just too much and I bottled it on the threshold. I told the others to go ahead and I would return to the bar we had just left. All three were curious, but Richard very generously opted to stay with me. The youngsters went down the steps and as Richard and I turned to leave I noted that, just as on mine and Tony's first visit, a hush had descended on the bar. Thirty yards up the road I could hear the bar conversation strike up again and I took this as a sign that Sion had just ordered the first Zagorka. They joined us again about forty minutes later, their curiosity satisfied. I asked them what they thought of it and Lucy was about to say something suitably sentimental when Sion cut across her. "I can just see the two of you sitting there…. with all the other old farts. Just like the Fox at home really."

As the evening wore on it seemed the order of the day to increasingly talk rubbish, something we were all quite good at with Richard taking the lead. He seems to just have an endless supply of anecdotes many of them from his rather dodgy past. We heard tales of a very dubious gang known as the carpet baggers and of some other associate of Richard's who was so evil he could kill a man with a spoon. I doubted the literal truth of many of the stories, but they were certainly entertaining. Finally we stumbled onto the subject of boxing and Richard trumped the stories I was telling by informing us that he had been asked not to return to his local boxing club as the trainer had deemed him too violent. Finally we returned to the hotel, fittingly one where Tony and I had usually stayed. I dimly remember us all sitting in the hotel lobby cum bar having a final nightcap and looking at the array of clocks giving the time from all around the world. My last memory of that evening was the four of us trying for ten minutes to work out what the time was in Bulgaria. We failed and so I am unable to report at what time we finally went to bed although I do recall it was one in the afternoon in Sydney.

Friday 2nd April 2010

Back in Veliko Tarnovo we had been invited to Nicky and Dima's house for dinner a sure sign, I am relieved to say, that there were no hard feelings about my less than chivalrous behaviour a few days earlier. Desi had also been invited and so the last piece of the who's who jigsaw could be put in place for Sion. I have described Nicky's living room in the past as like you might find in a giant's castle and now my fellow travellers could see what I had meant. As usual whole trees were roaring on the huge open fire and Lucy, who was sitting closest was starting to overheat. As in the past with Tony, Nicky was showing Richard his gun collection and as before I as a vegetarian was excluded from this. Sion seemed uninterested in anything other than the Rakia bottle. As before when Tony and I had been invited the meal proceeded incredible slowly with the main emphasis on smoking and drinking. When it did come the main course was gargantuan and we all returned to our various abodes well fed and well watered, especially Sion.

Monday 5th April 2010

To complete the experience I had planned to spend the last night in Sofia. We checked in to the same hotel where Tony and I had liked to stay. It was a huge hotel with a casino attached, reportedly frequented by gangsters. Over the years Tony and I had certainly seen a number of characters who fitted the profile. Just by reception there was a burly looking character with a shaven head standing in a sort of one man kiosk below a sign saying "Gold bought for cash".

That evening I took my friends and daughter for a meal to a beautiful courtyard restaurant just off the main city centre. As always I got temporarily lost trying to find it, but we got there eventually. Something you need to get used to if you eat out in Bulgaria is that food is delivered to the table as it comes out of the kitchen and as a result one person can receive their starter and then their main course before their friends have had anything. Equally you can order fish, fried potatoes and vegetables and receive the various elements of your meal with twenty minute intervals between each item. This does not matter to Bulgarians because when a dish arrives they show no interest and never start it until it has stood for at least half an hour. Therefore eventually everything that anyone has ordered is on the table. Richard in particular had never got used to this and it was unfortunate that it was him that suffered the final ignominy. Having eaten in some sort of order his salad, main course and dessert he was finally presented with a steaming plate of carrots.

We returned to the hotel with the intention of having a last drink in the night club on the top storey of the hotel. We entered the lobby and as before the shaven headed gentleman stood below the "Gold bought for cash" sign. But something had obviously taken place in our absence because he stood motionless as before, but now he sported two enormous black eyes.

We got into the lift, something I try to avoid in Bulgaria, and more with hope than expectation I pressed the button to transport us to the thirteenth floor. The old lift clanked into life and set about its long journey at a leisurely pace. At first I held my breath, but had I continued to do so I would have asphyxiated as the ride took about three minutes. Sion and Richie seemed unperturbed, but Lucy as always picking up on my anxiety started to turn white. However, we arrived unscathed.

We entered the night club to find a six piece live band playing to an empty room. You get used to this type of scenario in Bulgaria so it was no surprise, at least not to me. They were playing an excruciating Bulgarian folk song with the male and female singers wailing at each other. I think the song told one of those stories where the prince is turned into a frog and the woman becomes a swan with them being reunited when the swan eats the frog or something like that. Anyway it was awful, but fun. As we were the only audience they soon picked up that we were British and in a vain attempt to please us went into what they assumed was a British classic: 'Please Release Me' from Engelbert Humperdinck.

When they had finished we applauded appreciatively, but then fearing they might know Engelbert's whole back catalogue we approached them to make a request. After a long negotiation they seemed to understand what we wanted. We sat back in our seats as they struck up again: "Please release me, let me go." We looked at each other. Had the request been too obscure or did they simply not understand English very well? We decided to make it easier and looking at the ages of the band members we settled on 'anything from the Rolling Stones'. When they had completed their second rendition of Engelbert's classic I approached the band alone. I thought one person would be easier for them to handle. "Do you know the Rolling Stones?" I asked. "Da, da, of course." I was still not satisfied. "Does anyone speak German?" I ventured and they all looked at the female singer. "Sprechen Sie Deutsch?" I asked her and she confirmed that

171

she did with a confident answer in Bulgarian. Not knowing if there was any point I then repeated the request in German. "Irgendwas von den Rolling Stones, bitte." She nodded vigorously and turned to instruct the band. She took the mike, looked at the male singer and went straight into………… "Please release me, let me go. 'Cos you don't love me any more-re." That was our last request and the end of our last night in Bulgaria.

All the time we had been away Sion had been making notes. I thought this was him being conscientious in terms of learning about the business. How wrong can you be? His notes had been for a poem he was writing about our exploits. Sitting at the restaurant on the last night he had revealed all and read us the following poem, which I have reproduced in full with his kind permission:

Four Pilgrims – Sion Evans

In Manchester we begin our plight,

Where four pilgrims travel, for six long nights.

To warmer climes and foreign shores,

Where one has travelled many times before.

We land; Geoff's leadership does immediately begin,

We nearly loose him under a bus five minutes in!

One leftward glance and almost a sticky end,

As EasyJet collect his glasses once again.

Our bus rolls on into the Bulgarian countryside,

I sit tentatively, Richard by my side.

He causes my stress and worried looks,

With tales of wrong axels and rusty wheel nuts.

To Veliko Tarnovo our bus is bound,

Where fifteen Zagorkas are democratically downed.

And a decade of friendship is nearly undone,

By a few more Zagorka and a slurred 'I'm gone!'

Off to Varna with more bus dreads,

To currency exchanging drug dealers and birds nest heads.

Where our four travellers with no reason or rhyme,

Could bring themselves to tell the time!

Back to the giant's house and a meal that won't end,

A few Rakia and I'm talking bollocks again.

As Lucy glows by the fire that's roaring,

As we start to fear we will be there till morning.

Nikki our giant is doing the cooking,

Even after a handshake that left him wincing.

I wonder if the weapons would be as freely forthcoming,

If Nikki knew Richard was a man too violent for boxing.

To Sofia now as our journey's end looms,

With memories of carpet baggers and lethal spoons.

Our deals are done, our business is set,

After six beer filled nights I will never forget.

Back to Britain to the cold and damp,

After six whole nights avoiding the clamp.

Back to our homes to sleep in our beds,

With no fear of waking with a right angled head.

And when I sit by the Fox fire's glow,

Next to Brian and his little wife, Mo.

I won't stop smiling as Geoff calls the meeting to order,

As I hear 'Forget the group, let's have a Zagorka!'

Friday 25th June 2010

On 4th June I had received an email from Georgi saying he had sold the small apartment in Varna. The buyer had given him a holding deposit of two thousand leva and so the sale was secure. This was great news as it meant that the company was now in profit. I had adjusted the power of attorney held by Rada so that she could now sell property on our behalf. Therefore I had no need to travel to Bulgaria to complete the deal and today Rada had duly done that for me. I was now able to give everyone a dividend equivalent to twelve percent of their original stake which had already been returned to them. Also there was still the money from the eventual sale of the Veliko Tarnovo properties to come, although the market there, as elsewhere in Europe, was now slowing rapidly. Nevertheless they were there in the bank for the future. I was happy and wished Tony had been there to share the moment.

2011: New Beginnings

Tuesday 24ᵗʰ May 2011

It was a few years since Marieluise had accompanied me to Bulgaria and we decided that this year we would have a proper holiday there. We had been having beach type holidays in Spain and Greece for the last few years and so decided as a change we would head for Veliko Tarnovo. We both liked it there and we would be able to stay in 34, Gurko Street which she had never seen in its renovated state. Remembering what it was like before she had to trust me that it was now a really lovely little house. She took the chance. Coming to VT would also give me an opportunity to review the condition of the two properties and discuss any possible changes to drive forward the sales. In truth I was aware that the housing market in Bulgaria, as elsewhere, had collapsed as a result of the worldwide recession. The advice I would get from Desi would be to just hang on and wait and I knew that I would take this advice. There was no imperative to do otherwise.

So today we had arrived at Sofia airport and following a now familiar trail had got a taxi to the bus station and a bus to Veliko Tarnovo. As usual the weather was glorious and as she was now fully in holiday mode Marieluise immediately took up my suggestion of a drink at the Humphrey Bogart bar. She seemed really pleased to be here. After a couple of drinks we made our way to the house in Gurko Street. Marieluise loved the place. Hard as she tried she could not work out from the current layout of the house how it had looked before. In the end she gave up trying and just appreciated the house for what it was.

We had as always been working hard at Silver Rake, looking after three horses and maintaining the place through a hard winter. On top of that I had in February taken over as landlord of the Fox in Ysceifiog. A few months earlier the previous landlords had failed to see eye to eye with the owner of the pub regarding a new lease and the pub had closed. It was a disaster for the village and for its regulars of which I was one. On top of that Tony's words were ringing in my ears: "It's our pub; they [the landlords] are just passing through." I felt he was looking down on me wondering when I would make my move. After discussion between me, Sion, Marieluise and Kay we decided that if the owner would agree Sion and I would run it with Marieluise and Kay helping with cleaning, making fires etc. I approached the owner and offered him a fraction of what he was looking for as rent, but on the clear understanding that as soon as someone came forward as a potential tenant I would hand the pub over immediately. The owner and I were quite clear that we were doing this for our mutual benefit to get the pub open again. I hope Tony was satisfied.

Two months after taking on the Fox, on 31st March, I had retired after thirty nine years in child care social work. So with Sion left in charge of the Fox Marieluise and I were here for a well-earned rest. As always when we go on holiday I had an itinerary planned, but it included lots of time to just sit in the sun with a book and a glass of something and relax.

Wednesday 25th May 2011

After a day of not doing very much we had arranged to have a drink with Dima, Nicky and Desi at the bar at the top of town that had long since become their local. Having said that now they were parents their social life had been somewhat curtailed, although on this occasion Neda was staying with her Nan and so they were free for the evening. My business with Desi did not take very long. She gave me the advice regarding the houses that I had anticipated and I took the advice. Nicky and Dima had been keeping an eye on both places and they were able to tell us that Tunel Street remained in excellent condition. Regarding the house in Gurko Street, we had been able to see this for ourselves.

I told them about my early retirement which they approved of and then about becoming landlord of the Fox which surprised and intrigued them. Desi saw this as just access to free beer and although I tried to tell her there was a bit more to it than that she remained firmly of the opinion that Sion and I would be steadily drinking the profits. Unfortunately, so far there had been no profits to drink.

We got onto discussion about the recession and Nicky told us that, as in the UK, the building trade had been hit hard and, given the friendly invasion by the British had come to an end at the same time, he was struggling for work. Like a number of builders at home he had taken to buying very old properties in need of renovation and doing them up to sell or for rent. It was a way of keeping himself and his men working whilst creating some income. As the businessman he is he then told us that he had just finished work on a Renaissance style house in a village near Gabrovo. He said the location in the mountains was very special and we would definitely like it. Marieluise and I had come here for a relaxing holiday with no thoughts about property deals of any kind. However, Nicky can be very persuasive and before we knew it an arrangement had been made for us to visit the house with them the following morning.

Thursday 26th May 2011

Nicky and Dima picked us up outside the house in Gurko Street. Nicky could not have been doing that badly because the old Mercedes had been upgraded to a newer model. It was a comfortable car with the added bonus that we no longer had to stop every five miles to top up on water. We took the Stara Zagora road and after about ten miles filtered onto the road to Gabrovo. About five miles before Gabrovo we turned off onto what was little more than a dirt track. It had at some stage in the distant past been a tarmac road, but there was only patchy evidence of this. Eventually we came to a small, very small, village known as Todorcheta. Some of the houses were in quite good condition while others seemed deserted. This was not unusual in Bulgaria. Almost all of the houses were built in the style associated with the period of National Revival, the Renaissance. Eventually Nicky drew up outside one of the larger houses in the village. "Is this it?" I enquired and Dima confirmed that it was indeed. To say that we were impressed with the house was an understatement, although we were careful not to give the impression that we had any long term interest in the place. We were on holiday, not looking for houses and we had been careful to make this clear.

The house was quite large with three good size bedrooms, a living room with a kitchen attached and an enormous bathroom. Under the house the same amount of space was available for storage. There was a large yard flagged with stones that had originally been roof stones. In the yard there was a pagoda made with old roof beams and Nicky had started to train a vine to grow over it to provide shade for sitting out. The best feature was a veranda also made from old roof timbers that was the length of the house. As always, Nicky had done a wonderful job of renovating the place. It looked like an old house that had just been built if that is not a contradiction. He was very proud of the place and determined to spark our interest, but we were determined not to bite.

About five miles away there was an historic village, Bojentsi that had received European funding to renovate all the buildings which, like the houses in Todorcheta, were built in the Renaissance style. This gave us a good impression of how Todorcheta would have looked in its heyday. There were two or three very nice restaurants in Bojentsi and we choose one where we could sit outside shaded by trees. It was a truly lovely setting, the sun was shining and the food and the company was good.

When we got back to Veliko Tarnovo and had said goodbye to Nicky and Dima we could not stop talking about the house in Todorcheta. There was no good hiding it; we were smitten.

2014: Summer Visitors: Working Vacations

14-17th June 2014

Today, 14th June, we received our first visitor from home, my brother Roy. He came by plane, taxi and finally bus and having followed my instructions to the letter, he arrived happy and on time without being fleeced by anyone, particularly the Sofia taxi drivers. It was great to see him and although he was tired having got up long before dawn, we still managed to spend a very pleasant evening sitting outside exchanging news and downing Zagorkas. Obviously we had more to tell him than vice-versa, but it was still nice to hear news from home. It is strange how all the things that consume your thoughts when at home get quickly forgotten due to new and different priorities, but once you start talking about them again they instantly take on their old importance. Roy was amazed at what we had achieved in terms of getting everything straight for us and the horses, but came here knowing that there was loads left to do and he was more than willing to help.

Two issues were currently consuming us: firstly, how to get the field opposite the house fully functional for the horses and secondly the need to get a wood supply for our winter fuel. In many ways the two issues crossed over in that I still had many trees to fell in the field and these could be sawn and chopped to contribute to our wood stash. After some discussion we decided that Roy and I would set about felling the trees with a vengeance and would saw those and the ones I had chopped down earlier into manageable logs. Having little experience in these matters I found it hard to estimate how much wood I would have from my own resources and how much I would need to order. We therefore decided that we would play it safe and order ten cubic metres of wood, probably enough for the winter in itself, and regard the wood we produced as a bonus that would surely get used at some time.

The following morning I was pleasantly surprised to see Roy up and ready for action. We did a few hours before breakfast as I had already learned that this was the best time to get things done before the heat became unbearable. Marieluise had drawn the same conclusion regarding riding and on this morning as on previous ones she and her new riding pal, Mandi, were in the saddle before eight o clock. As it turned out this one and the next few days were cooler than of late and whereas I regretted this with regard to Roy's holiday it was so much easier to work.

Over the next few days we worked very hard and I have to admit that there were times when I was ready to call it a day, but Roy would encourage me to keep going. In my defence I have had to work like this almost every day since we arrived to get things ship-shape whereas for Roy it represents a very different way of life and he was clearly enjoying the new challenge. By the middle of the week the field was for the first time starting to look like a field and we also had an almighty stash of wood. It was too late though; I had already ordered the ten cubic metres and it was due to arrive tomorrow.

Regarding this wood I had received some very Bulgarian advice. The basis of the advice was as follows: People selling the wood are always looking to rip you off so you must order it in metre length logs so that you can clearly identify that you have received the quantity you paid for. If you allow them to deliver the wood ready for use they will sell you a cubic metre or so short. This completely ignores the fact that you then leave yourself about three or four days' work and there is no doubt that you would also use several gallons of expensive chainsaw fuel in the process. I had ignored this advice and ordered the wood ready to use. If they are to become a more harmonious society Bulgarians must somehow shake off this overwhelming belief that most people are out to rob or fiddle you and try to trust each other more. We will see what tomorrow's delivery brings.

Wednesday 18ᵗʰ June 2014

As promised the wood delivery arrived at ten thirty. In typical Bulgarian style, instead of a tipper truck, the wood was brought in a large transit van that was completely unsuited for the task. To add to their woes the entrance to our yard is short and very steep. Given the weight of the load the back end of the transit was almost on the road so as soon as the driver tried to back up the van ran aground. As a result the wood had to be emptied out about six metres short of our gate. I went forward to help, but soon realised I would be taking my life in my hands. The driver and his mate opened the back door and a mass of small logs tumbled out. Then with their backs to the gate they started to throw the wood through their legs into or at least in the direction of the gate. They had obviously practiced this routine many times and there were simply logs flying everywhere. Any attempt to help or clear the pile while they were still throwing would have been suicidal. We had no option but to stand and watch in awe.

After about forty minutes the van was empty and we had an enormous pile of logs blocking our gateway. Across the logs one of the guys informed me that this was five cubic metres and they would be back with the other five in about two hours. This meant that we had to get this load away and stacked before they returned; a tall order. We set about it with Marieluise filling, me barrowing – using two barrows – and Roy stacking. We had just finished when we heard the overworked transit labouring up the hill.

When they arrived with the second load I think they expected to find us in a state of chaos and distress surrounded by tumbling logs. Roy had done a very professional job of stacking and all three of us tried to look pleased with ourselves although I am sure that the overwhelming impression we gave was of complete exhaustion. Again the van ran aground and again the two delivery men went through the same pantomime leaving us after about an hour – they were definitely slowing – in the same unenviable position. This time we just did enough to be able to get the gates closed and against all Bulgarian advice left about four cubic metres outside the gate for any Tom, Dick or Gypsy to pinch. Unfortunately the next morning it was still there.

Half of our wood delivery stacked and ready for the winter

On returning to the UK my youngest daughter, Lucy, asked Roy if he had had a good time. "As boot camps go it was quite OK really!" was his cryptic reply. I hope he was joking.

Thursday 17ᵗʰ July 2014

Today we anticipated the arrival of our friend Richard from Wales. As mentioned before Rich owns a large plant hire business with trucks, diggers, dumpers etc. It was he who went over the truck with a fine tooth comb before we set off and thankfully gave me practical tuition on tyre changing which I put to good use in Romania.

This time Richard is coming to relax a bit following some setbacks with his work, but also to do me yet another favour: sort out the field I have rented so that it can be used for horses. Nikki is a great builder and in the period leading up to our arrival he converted our outbuildings to stables and did a superb job. However when it comes to clearing fields, a job he also undertook, he is nowhere near as accomplished. His reliance on manpower – i.e. the Lost Boys – means that his ability to turn an overgrown orchard into a paddock is very restricted. Add to that the fact that he knows little about horses and it is not surprising that the field he delivered to us as "finished" is barely fit for goats, let alone horses. It remains covered in weeds, with some vicious slopes that need to be levelled out. Over the last several weeks I have been cutting down more trees, but a digger is required to carry out the job. Richie wanted me to hire a self-drive mini digger and a dumper so that he, with my assistance on the dumper could create a paddock from the wilderness that is the field. I have spent endless hours asking local people and surfing the net to get what he said we needed. However, I have had to tell him that there are no dumpers in Bulgaria and with the exception of one half-witted Englishman who owns an ancient one and a half ton digger and lives two hundred miles away there are no self-drive diggers for hire.

I knew Richard would find this hard to accept and so it came as no surprise that once I had picked him up at the airport and we had reached the main road he started to question whether it really was the case that there was nothing available. All I had managed to arrange was a ten ton digger driven by an English speaking Bulgarian called Svetoslav. He had been available for weeks now and keen to start, but I had delayed him so that I could at least use Richard's expertise to direct and supervise him.

After a pleasant car journey during which I relayed to Richard some of the stories chronicled here we arrived home. Like most people who come to see us, Richie was taken aback at just how lovely the place is. Since being here we have got the weeds under control, planted numerous flowers, revived old plants and trained our vine to screen one of our designated sitting areas. We have bought two sets of garden furniture and erected a gazebo on an elevated part of the yard. As a result the impression as you come through the gate is a very pleasing one and Richard was certainly impressed. However, I know him well enough to understand that more than anything he wanted to see the field where the work was to be undertaken and so even before he had a cup of tea I took him across. Given that he knew how much work Nicky had done clearing the field I do not think he expected it to be so bad. Richie has great expertise when it comes to ground work and so my heart sank when he told me quite simply that we had the wrong machine for the job. The biggest problem was that the field was so slopping that a machine on wheels would struggle, whereas a mini digger is on tracks and would negotiate the terrain without difficulty. In my naïveté I had thought that given the size of the task, the bigger the machine the better. However, none of this made any difference as I had hired the only machine that I could find and he was due to start on Saturday, i.e. in two days' time.

After much discussion we decided that Svetoslav would come on Saturday as arranged and, to use Richie's words "knock the field about a bit". Following that Rich was still determined to get a self-drive mini digger on site. Predictably he made me trawl the internet again and at last he could see for himself that the options were poor to non-existent. As I had done weeks earlier, he spoke to a British bloke called Paul who lived four hours away. He had a very small digger and informed Rich that "Where the machine goes, Paul goes." The self-same phrase he had used to me. So enchanted was Richie by Paul's lack of helpfulness I had to extract the phone from him before he said something libellous. This left the Englishman, Tim, who lived near the Black Sea coast and was the proud owner of an ancient mini digger. It was an old, slow digger, it weighed only one and a half tons and I would have to pay for it to be transported half way across Bulgaria. Given the limitations of the machine it was also very expensive to hire. Although I had dismissed this as not economic, Richie was determined. Although he acknowledged that it was old, crap, and expensive he wanted it. After a brief conversation with Tim that only confirmed all the above, Rich told me to order it. Tim agreed to have the machine here at nine on Monday morning after Svetoslav had done what he could over the weekend. It was all very unsatisfactory, but the best that Bulgaria could offer. Also I was being reminded that whereas for most of us we need to breathe to live, Richie must dig to live. We left it at that and I distracted Richie the only way I could; by producing a crate of beer. Soon we all settled down and Rich went to bed with a smile on his face, despite his dissatisfaction with the arrangements.

Saturday 19th July 2014

Finally the day for digging dawned and as promised Svetoslav arrived in his machine at nine o clock prompt. I introduced him to Richard and as I introduced him I gave Svetoslav a bit of background regarding Richard and his plant hire company. He seemed a bit intimidated. However, Richard could not have been nicer and soon they were discussing together how the job could be approached. Within five minutes Svetoslav's machine was working with Richard and me looking on. I thought Richard would stay observing for some time and I was just wondering how the driver would feel about this when Richard spoke my thoughts. "That'll do. The lad obviously knows what he is doing. Anyway all digger drivers hate being watched! We'll come back in an hour and see how he is getting on." I was impressed and much relieved on Svetoslav's behalf.

Richard pulled out a chair for some serious sunbathing while I went back to helping Marieluise with the horses. Marieluise asked me to rasp the horses' feet which was a daily task that we had been undertaking since arriving in Bulgaria to make up for the lack of a trusted farrier. It is hard on the back and so the job usually fell to me. Flo was being a bit difficult and while I was rasping one of her hind feet she pulled hard with her leg. As I have done many times before I continued to hold on to her leg. She usually gives up when you do that whereas if you let go she just learns bad habits. I can only assume that I usually somehow ride the movement of her leg whereas this time I seemed to absorb it. The next thing I knew I was writhing on the floor in pain. Richard ran across thinking I had been kicked, but the horse had not touched me. In fact, she was studying my prostrate form trying to work out just what had happened. Marieluise came up with the practical suggestion that I should get up as I was lying immediately behind Flo's feet. I attempted to comply with this eminently sensible suggestion, but found I could not move. The muscle in the back of my thigh had somehow taken all the force from the movement of Flo's leg and gone into spasm. Eventually the pain subsided slightly and I got to my feet, but could barely walk. Given all the things that needed to be done this was not good timing. Somehow I hobbled into the house and sat there in a state of desolation.

After about four hours Svetoslav had made a big impression on the site and had moved down to the lower level when, despite forecasts to the contrary, the heavens opened and it lashed down with rain. Soon we were engulfed in a full blown electric storm and Svetoslav struggled to get his machine back to the higher level. We all agreed to call it a day and Richard and I offered to take him home so that he could leave his machine here to hopefully continue tomorrow. I got gingerly into the driver's seat, but found that operating the clutch was completely beyond me. Richard for reasons I won't go into did not have his licence with him, but nevertheless had to drive. We at once resolved that our trip to Gabrovo would have to take in a visit to A&E.

Svetoslav directed Richie to his home which took us through the centre of town. The rain had not abated and the roads were literally like rivers. This happens every time there is exceptional rainfall as the drainage system just cannot cope. Sometimes as on this occasion water pumps out of the drains rather than pouring into them. An added danger driving in such conditions is that the driver can no longer see where the numerous holes are in the road. After a short but hazardous journey we arrived at Svetoslav's home, an apartment in a high- rise on the other side of Gabrovo. As he was getting out Svetoslav asked me if I knew where the hospital was. Although I had at first had some idea, the trip to his house coupled with the debilitating effect of the pain in my leg had left me completely at sea. Without hesitating he got into his own car and told us to follow him. Ten minutes later we arrived at the hospital.

I got out of the car and went over to thank Svetoslav, but as far as he was concerned his mission was not yet complete. Accompanying me into the hospital he explained to the staff what had happened. On their instructions he then took me in the lift up three storeys to the orthopaedic department. There he again explained to the specialist what the trouble was and without delay she set about

187

diagnosing the problem. A thorough examination then took place during which Svetoslav's main function was to ask me "Does that hurt?" and relay my answer back to the doctor, although the expression on my face probably relayed the answers fairly effectively. After about ten minutes I was informed that I had a muscle spasm. The doctor prescribed painkillers and a muscle relaxant and we were on our way. I had entered the hospital only fifteen minutes earlier and the job was already complete. This certainly compared most favourably with my experiences at A&E in the UK.

Having taken us this far, Svetoslav was determined to finish the job. He led the way to a duty chemist, went in with me, and translated the dosage instructions etc. The man was a star. Richard offered him some money for his time and fuel, but he would have none of it. Just another example of why one must never make generalisations about people based on national stereotypes. Svetoslav was a decent and kind man by any definition. Richard drove me home and it was obvious that he too was having to rearrange some of his prejudices about Eastern Europeans. It reminded me of something I had once heard Tony Benn relate. His son Hilary had just returned from a gap year travelling and was confronted by a characteristic question from his father. "So son, what have you learned?" Hilary gave the question some thought as he had no doubt learned to do. "We are all the same. People everywhere are just the same."

Monday 21st July

So today we were expecting Tim-nice-but-dim to deliver the ancient, underweight mini-digger so that Richard could finish the job. At eight thirty we were ready and waiting for the digger to be delivered. At nine thirty we were still waiting. At ten thirty we tried ringing Tim, but got no answer. We then tried ambushing him by using another phone, but this did not work. Fifteen minutes later we tried again, but this time his phone was switched off and it remained switched off for the rest of the morning. We left loads of messages and texts, but none were returned. Eventually even Richard admitted defeat. Why someone would advertise a self-drive mini-digger, make an arrangement to bring it and then not show is frankly beyond me, but that is what happened. Finally, we went back to the ever helpful Svetoslav and asked if he knew anyone with a mini-digger. This was a bit cheeky as we had originally taken him on to do the whole job, but he did not seem to be upset by this. Ten minutes later he rang back and said a friend of his could do it, but it would be man and machine. This was a bit of a blow to Richard, but he had by now virtually come to terms with the fact that Bulgarians do not do self-drive hire. What he did find hard to accept however was the news that the guy could not do the work until the following week. Richard had come to dig, or at least to supervise the job and was ultimately left frustrated. I could see that crates of Zagorka would have to play a big role in placating him and so it proved.

2011: Viewing the Future

Tuesday 6ᵗʰ September 2011

As I was now retired there was nothing to stop me coming to Bulgaria for longer than a week, this being the normal length of my stay, so this time I had decided to stay for a month. I knew that because of her attachment to her horses there was no way Marieluise would stay that long and I had made plans accordingly. Marieluise would come with me and stay for a fortnight and during that second week our daughter Lucy would join us. I would then take them back to the airport together and pick up my brother, Roy. He would stay for a week and then after a few days on my own I would return home.

Once we had decided on these arrangements there was only one place that Marieluise and I wanted to stay and that was in the house in Todorcheta. I had been in touch with Dima several months back who had confirmed that they had done nothing with the house and so we had made arrangements to stay there. So today we had arrived in Sofia, hired a car and made our way to Todorcheta. The place was as beautiful as we had remembered it and we were both very excited to be here. Although it was already early evening we had decided to do some exploring on foot to get to know our surroundings. From the main road that went from VT to Gabrovo we had noted that the road to the village went up and up, round two hairpin bends until one reached the first few houses. Almost immediately after that there was a small village centre at which point the road split into two, one heading left and down and the other bearing right and continuing uphill. Our house was situated up the hill, about sixty metres from the village centre.

First of all we walked to the end of our road which eventually petered out to a track and then came to an abrupt halt just past the last house. However before we got to the end we had noticed a number of footpaths leading off the road and we made a mental note to explore them in the next few days. We then turned around headed back past the house to the centre of the village and then proceeded down the path that lead to the rest of the village. Again the road came to an end, but beyond it was a path leading into the forest. This looked really interesting and we resolved to come back in the days following to see where it came out.

Finally we headed back to the main road and crossed it to have a look at the village on the opposite side of the road, Rahovtsi. As I looked across the road I saw some tables and chairs with people sitting around chatting in the early evening sunshine. From a distance I could not make out if I was looking into someone's garden, but as I got closer my prayers were answered. There was a little bar just above what I took to be the village square and it was easy walking distance from Todorcheta. Rejoice! We walked towards the bar and as I realised that the whole clientele were men I started to sense reluctance on Marieluise's part to stop there. But help was at hand. Just as she hesitated a man in his sixties appeared from nowhere and pointed the way, quite assertively to the bar. "Well, it would be churlish to shun such ardent hospitality." I said with a grin and before Marieluise could refuse I had ordered two drinks from the old lady that appeared to be running the place. I now knew where I would be spending the early evenings during my luxuriously long vacation. I was beginning to like this place more and more.

Saturday 1st October 2011

After a fabulous month spent at Todorcheta firstly with Marieluise, then Lucy and finally with my brother Roy, I was at Sofia airport waiting for my flight home. Except for the fact that I was now missing Marieluise and wanting to see her, I would have happily stayed much longer. I had spoken in principle to Nicky and Dima and they would be only too happy if we took the house on permanently, although as things stood this was a long way from being possible. Now that I was retired I would happily live here for half the year and at Silver Rake the other half, but obviously I only wanted to do this together with Marieluise and she would never leave her horses for more than a month, tops. I thought about all the possible permutations for trying to make my dream possible, but there was no solution. My wife needed to be with her horses; there was no getting round that basic fact, or was there?

2014: Final Stories from a Quirky Country

Tuesday 29th July 2014

For more than a week now, Marieluise has been complaining that her ear is bunged up and closed and she cannot hear properly. She had some drops from the chemist, but they have done nothing to alleviate the condition. Since we have been in Bulgaria there have been at least two occasions when, had she been at home, Marieluise would have visited her GP, but since being here she has shown a distinct aversion to medical intervention. Today we were on our way to collect our laundry from Dryanovo and I insisted that she go to the little community hospital where a GP is usually on duty. I frightened her into it by saying she may partially lose her hearing if she does not seek help. She eventually agreed and soon we found ourselves on the second floor outside the doctor's surgery.

A noticeable thing with all public services in Bulgaria is that there is almost never any form of reception. The same applies in this hospital. You enter at the ground floor and are just left to work out for yourself where to find what you are looking for. We found ourselves on the second floor by a process of elimination, i.e. there was nobody and no sounds of life on the first two floors so we just kept going up until we found someone. Then you sit outside the closed door of the doctor's surgery and wait until the previous patient spills out. The first time the door opened we foolishly awaited a summons from the doctor that never came and sensing our hesitation a woman who came after us went in and shut the door behind her. This woman and a man that we presumed to be the doctor then spent ten minutes shouting at each other and therefore as the door opened Marieluise again hesitated this time through fear rather than as a result of not knowing the protocol. However, gaining strength from the fact that the woman came out laughing she at last entered with me accompanying her in case of the need for an interpreter, although I had only about a ten percent better chance of understanding than she did. There was only one person in the room, a man in his fifties wearing jeans and a tee shirt. Thankfully he had the tell-tale sign of a stethoscope around his neck and when I addressed him as "Doctor" he did not demur.

As usual my first question was "Do you speak English?" and as I had expected the answer "Ne!" came back at once. I had prepared for this with the dubious help of Google Translate and so immediately went into action. "Ukhoto si e zapushena –zatvoren. Ne mozhe da se chuva dobre." This should mean "Her ear is clogged – closed. Cannot hear properly." It appeared that I had got it reasonably correct because he picked up a small torch and invited Marieluise to sit down in his patient's chair. This chair must have been ancient. It was a small upright metal chair covered on the seat, back and arms with worn black leather. It also had a belt to strap the patient in at the waist. The one and only time I have seen anything similar was in a small dentistry museum in Dumfries. .The chair displayed there is said to be over one hundred years old. He must have wrongly assessed Marieluise as brave because he made no use of the straps. He shone his torch down Marieluise's ear and gave a knowing laugh. Immediately he went into action. He put a tea towel on her shoulder, drew about a pint of water out of the kettle with a giant metal syringe and gave me an old enamel kidney dish to hold under her ear, laughingly referring to me as his "assistant". He then shot the whole pint into her ear and as her first scream subsided he reloaded his syringe and repeated the action.

"Chuvate po-dobre?" He asked her if she could hear better now. Marieluise nodded dumbly, forgetting that a nod in Bulgaria often means no. The doctor picked up his syringe again and headed for the kettle. "No, no more!" she yelled. "My ear is OK!" The doctor stopped in his tracks and looked uncertain. He understood that she had had enough, but was still unsure whether her hearing had been restored. "Chuvate dobre." I told him she could hear fine now and he smiled and then started to chuckle again as if the whole thing had been a tremendous jape. "Dvadeset leva!" he beamed. I paid him his twenty leva and as Marieluise stumbled from the room he began to laugh uncontrollably. He did not stop even when the next patient entered the surgery. Outside Marieluise jumped into the car and asked me to get her away from the butcher of Dryanovo as quickly as possible. "Are you OK?" I asked tentatively. "Stop bloody shouting!" she replied. The butcher's work had obviously been a success.

Friday 19th September 2014

Earlier in the summer I had changed our company address from Varna to Veliko Tarnovo. We no longer own any property in Varna so it seemed to make sense. Eventually however I realised that as a result I would have to change the registration of the car to Veliko Tarnovo as well. When this dawned on me I was desolate, remembering only too well how horrendous it had been when I had undertaken this task in Varna despite the able assistance rendered by Nicky and Dima. To make matters worse Dima now worked full time so I could not look to her for help. Today I finally bucked up the courage to go ahead and set off in the car to Veliko Tarnovo accompanied by a Bulgarian friend, Detelin, known as 'Dido'. I had met Dido at the garage where I have my car serviced. He is a friend of the owner and speaks excellent English. He is also an interesting and amusing man and I knew that if the registration took all day, as I expected, I would at least enjoy his company.

Our first task was to go to the trade registration office and collect a copy of my new company registration documents. This appeared to be going well until the time came to pay the seven leva for the new document. Naively I offered the young woman seven leva in cash, but she told me she could not accept this. I offered a visa card, but this too was unacceptable. No, the required method of payment was to go to a bank with the trade registration agency's account number and complete a bank transfer. The first bank we went to did not do transfers, but the second one did. It took about twenty minutes in the bank and involved three members of staff, the first to complete the transfer slip, the duty manager to sign his authorisation and the cashier to receive the money and give me a receipt. Dido took all of this in his stride and after being charged three leva to transfer seven leva we returned to the trade agency to receive the company document. Step one was now completed and it had only taken just over an hour.

We returned to the car and drove to the traffic police centre where the car was to be registered, but not before I had taken a wrong turning into a drive thru cash and carry that I could not get out of until it became my turn to tell the customer service person that I did not actually want anything and had only joined the queue for fun. When we parked at the traffic police centre I was at least relieved to see that there was no mile long queue as I had experienced in Varna. Dido asked me for my documents and we boldly approached the first desk to be told they were just closing for lunch and to come back at one o clock. It was now ten to twelve.

Sitting in a nearby café I discovered that I had chosen well in asking Dido to accompany me. I was already wound up, but he showed a wonderful attitude to the whole affair that took all the stress out of the situation. "Geoff, by the end of the day your car will be registered and if it isn't we will just come back tomorrow. Don't panic, just enjoy your coffee sitting here in the sunshine." I could not really argue with that and I did indeed relax as Dido told me tale after tale from his life and about his friends and family. My favourite one was about his late father who he said was past his sell-by date and very forgetful in his final few years. His father's best friend was much the same. On one particular day his father and the old man's friend were sitting playing cards when they realised they were out of cigarettes. Dido's father, Vasil volunteered to go to the shop to get the ciggies and some matches. Knowing how forgetful he was he employed a clever means of remembering. As he walked he chanted "Cigarettes – matches – cigarettes – matches." in time with his footfall. When he arrived at the shop the shopkeeper was very pleased to see him. "Vasil, it's so long since I have seen you, how are you?" "I'm fine, thank you." Vasil replied. "And your boy, Dido, well I hope?" "Yes, very well," replied Dido's father. "Now, what can I get you?" enquired the shopkeeper. Vasil thought for a while. ""Oh yes, some sausage, please. He returned to his friend, brandishing his purchase. "You see, Vasil, you old goat" said his friend. "You're not so forgetful after all; you remembered the sausage."

At one o clock we returned to the fray and by now Dido's stress reduction techniques had worked wonders on me. "Just regard it as more material for your book." he said as we were told by the woman at counter number four that we should be at counter number six to speak to the man who had just sent us to her. Eventually the first phase of the administration was completed and we were told to drive the car into the technical area. Here a one minute technical inspection took place that involved the technician looking at two tyres – he could not see more without moving, staring at the engine and writing down the engine number. He signed some document that Dido had been given and we returned to the admin section, no doubt to be given more documentation.

Ten minutes later we were sent back to the technical area to have the Varna number plates removed. I assumed that they would now put the new ones on and it would be job done. No such luck. First of all the car had to be stripped of its current identity, a technique that Bulgarian bureaucracy often practiced on people, so I was told to park in a special half way zone and to go and surrender my current registration document to the authorities at window number three. Window number three was not staffed by an administrator, no this was a solemn matter requiring a police officer. He checked through the copious documents very carefully and sent us almost naked back to window number four with just one small tear off slip to our name. Here we would be furnished with a new registration document. It was only quarter to four and we were nearing the end, or so we thought. The woman at counter number four, showing no mercy or common humanity, told us to come back in an hour.

Back to the café for more stress reduction therapy from Dido. Luckily he had plenty more anecdotes in his locker. This time he told me about a friend who had linked up and eventually lived with an English woman. She was not pretty, Dido informed me with a grimace to emphasise this sad fact, but his friend was sure she was rich. She was after all English. Early on the friend had insured himself against the possible hardship of looking only at this woman. He had informed her that he had very sensitive eyes requiring him to wear sunglasses at all times. From behind these glasses he could at least look at Bulgarian women without his subterfuge being detected. Sadly she turned out to be poor as well as ugly and the friend now lives happily with a penniless, but beautiful Bulgarian girl.

At quarter to five we returned to the tyrannical occupier of window number four just in time for her to call out the names of ten successful applicants to collect their new documents. Alas, my name was not amongst them. Showing courage way beyond the miserly thirty leva I had promised him, Dido stepped forward. "Excuse me, madam. Is there any chance you have forgotten my English friend?" She barely looked at him, but instead rustled some papers still on her desk, picking one of them up by the corner as if it was covered in dog poo. "Is this him?" she asked holding the paper at a slant so that Dido had to bend his head sideways to read it. "Yes, Geoffrey Michael Hart is the name on your sheet and that is indeed my friend here." "Well, how I am supposed to read out a name like that, I have no idea." Nevertheless she handed my documents to Detelin, although what she would have made of me calling him Dido, I cannot imagine. Triumphantly we returned to the technical area holding our registration documents aloft and remained in the car while our glorious new number plates were attached. Home and dry!

Tuesday 7th October 2014

This evening my friend Keith and I paid a visit to our favourite haunt the Boriki bar, which is no more than a few tables and chairs outside the shop in the nearby village of Boriki. The sun was warm and the air was clear. The views from where we sit are magnificent. As far as we can we like to chat with the locals and one or two of the regulars speak quite good English. A local man called Vasco lived for a number of years in America and he often acts as interpreter between us and the other drinkers. On this particular evening the local writer and journalist, Velizar Velchev, to whom I have previously made reference came for a drink. Velizar wrote a short book entitled '7/8 The British Way' which includes material based on interviews and anecdotes from other British people living in the area. Obviously meeting him was of great interest to me, given this book and he was equally interested in what I was doing. He was a quiet man who spoke very little English and we were frustrated as we could not have the sort of in-depth conversation that we both wanted.

Enter stage left Vasco. We both assumed that Vasco would be able to translate for us so we bought him a beer, or to be more accurate Keith bought him a beer, and made room at our table. What we had not reckoned for was that this week the new season Rakia was ready and Vasco had been sampling it all afternoon. When I gave him a sentence to translate he sat back with a grand gesture of the arms and declared "This man, Velizar, is a great writer. He write books you know: 7/8 is great book. I have it at home." I tried again with even less success. "He no fool. He author. It in English, but not for Dummkopfs you understand." This was a rare excursion into the German vernacular that only went to underline his untapped potential as an interpreter. But tonight it was to remain untapped. In the end Velizar gave me a signed copy of his book with his phone number attached. When I contact him I will provide my own interpreter.

Wednesday 22nd October 2014

Today we took Flo in the horsebox to a friend's house near VT to use her ménage. Norma had said she would not be around, but her husband, Gordon, would be there. We arrived to be greeted by Gordon stripped to the waist wearing Bermuda shorts, and sandals. The temperature on the yard was twenty nine degrees Celsius. It was so hot Marieluise had difficulty getting Flo to concentrate and Marieluise herself, wearing a riding hat and a body protector was close to exploding. That evening we had a look at the weather forecast. This beautiful spell of autumn weather had so far lasted for two or three weeks and we were keen to know how long it would continue. Imagine our surprise when the forecast indicated that the temperature would drop by more than twenty degrees and on Saturday there would be up to four centimetres of snow. Uncharacteristically, we were off our guard and we did not take the forecast particularly seriously.

Saturday 25ᵗʰ October 2014

We should have taken the forecast *very* seriously. Today we woke up to a heavy snowfall and by the time we gathered ourselves it was already too late to get the car down the hill. However, the forecast had anticipated only an inch or so of snow so at first we were not too bothered, but as the day wound on and the snow continued to fall it became obvious that the forecast was hopelessly wrong. By two in the afternoon a foot of snow had fallen and we could no longer even see the road let alone drive on it. Nevertheless, we had prepared for bad weather at some point, although we had not expected anything like this until well into the winter. We had a freezer full of basic food as well as plenty of food for the horses and the dog. We had an old wood burning range to cook on and were heating the house with wood. We probably had enough fuel for two winters.

Then at two thirty in the afternoon the electricity went off and although it came on and off for the rest of the afternoon by five in the evening it was off and staying off. This is a particular problem for us as our water supply is pumped from our own well to the taps via two electric pumps, so we had no water. We had, however prepared for the water supply failing, although our main fear had been that in the hot weather the well would run dry. We had more than a thousand litres of rainwater in our tanks and about three hundred litres of well water in large plastic bottles under the house. So although life was set to become somewhat inconvenient, we were ready for whatever was thrown at us.

Sunday 26ᵗʰ October 2014

We woke up this morning and it was still snowing and we now had about eighteen inches of snow. At least there was no wind and therefore no drifting. At home in Wales such snowfalls are always accompanied by strong winds resulting in drifts up to six feet deep. Here without the drifts we found it remarkably easy to function outside. The horses had now been in the stables for twenty four hours and despite the conditions we decided to put their rugs on and put them out. The best field in such conditions is the one we own at the bottom of the village near the cemetery. It is the only one of our fields which is completely flat and therefore safe even in deep snow. Both horses love snow and as soon as we released them they ran around, rolled several times and generally enjoyed themselves. We carried water and hay nets down to the field so they had everything they needed for a few hours of fun.

There was still no electricity, no water and no internet and at about midday the phone network went down too. Most of our neighbours had fled to Gabrovo as soon as the snow started or even before so now, with no means of communication, we really were on our own. Were we bothered? Not in the least.

Tuesday 28th October 2014

We woke up this morning to our fourth day without any amenities or means of communication, but at least it had stopped snowing. We were now putting the horses out for the whole day and before we did anything else we set about organising this. Over breakfast we reviewed the plans we had put in place for such eventualities and felt quite pleased with ourselves. If we had made a mistake in our planning it was over-reliance on the freezer. Although we had put the freezer in the tack room it was now starting to thaw and as we are pretty fanatical about food hygiene we were facing losing some of the contents. As vegetarians nothing in there was valuable, but we did resolve that in future we would stock up on tinned and bottled food. There was always an infinite variety of the latter in Bulgarian shops. If we organised our food in this way and did everything else the same we reckoned we could manage for weeks, although whether it would ever get that desperate we did not know.

Suddenly at about two in the afternoon the power was restored and by five we had internet and a telephone line. The first thing we did was refill all the bottles of well water that we had used. Usually we are very careful with our use of the well, but it would be some time before we would have to worry about it drying up.

So this is how Bulgaria shapes up when there is a heavy fall of snow. Almost everyone left the village. The snow plough cleared the first part of the road to our village, but did not get as far as the first house. The power supply failed as did the internet connection and the telephone network and they all stayed off for the best part of four days. Even when we had a telephone connection we could not get through to the electricity company for up to date information despite many attempts. If this is the effect of a heavy snowfall then God help anyone who is not prepared when winter really kicks in. It was another reminder that, although the country is making steady progress on many fronts, Bulgaria is still unfinished business.

Thursday 6th November 2014

Today it is seven months since we arrived at our home in Todorcheta. We have worked incredibly hard, but it has been worth it. We now have all of our fields in use and we have at least some proper pasture land. The horses have become more and more accustomed to the flies, mosquitoes etc. and now the flies have virtually gone until next spring so life for the horses is easier. Inside the house we have bought a few bits and pieces to make it more like home and less like a holiday residence. With the winter in mind we have replaced our little pot-bellied stove in the living room with an enormous ten kilowatt wood burner. The little stove was cute, but again more suitable for holidays. I have also got the old wood fuelled cooker into use which will be handy if the electricity fails as it frequently does and will also contribute to the warmth of the house.

Certainly one of the biggest reasons for us coming here is the weather; we love to be outdoors and it is wonderful to have spent the whole summer in shorts and tee-shirts. It is an added bonus that, putting the freak snow storm aside, we are still enjoying beautiful sunshine in November. Marieluise is doing what she loves best, riding and looking after her horses. She goes for a long hack three or four times a week with our friend Mandi and now that Mandi's husband

Keith has joined her here I have someone to go for a pint with, which is an important ingredient in my all round happiness.

We both miss our family hugely and this is the only serious downside to the whole venture. People say to me all the time "You must miss your grandchildren" which I do, but more than anything I miss my daughters to whom I am very close. At home we had Emily just around the corner and Lucy, although living sixty miles away in Manchester came home to see us every week. Despite this we are glad that we have come here. We love and miss our family, but we are responsible for our own happiness and we are very happy. People ask you why you do things in life to which the answer should always be "Why not?" Every experience enhances your life and when I look back over all my adventures in this beautiful country I can only say there would have been a huge hole in my life had I never come here.

More than thirty percent of Bulgaria is woodland and at this time of year the countryside is breath-taking. I have never seen so many colours as in the forests surrounding us. As well as riding we have done a lot of walking and sometimes you have to just stop and stare at the wonderful views. In some directions you can look for miles without seeing any sign of habitation. Other times you see a tiny village nestling in a picturesque valley beneath the mountains, apparently miles from civilisation. The only downside to hiking are the maps and the signage. When we bought a map of our area designed for hikers and mountain bikers we were a little alarmed to see our own village placed on the wrong side of the main road. Since then we have never fully trusted the map and just as well, because sometimes it depicts the route of the paths accurately and sometimes it is way off. A few times we have found ourselves entering a small hamlet to which the map makes no reference.

On the more popular walks there are signs and markers just like at home, but often they take you into the depths of a forest or to the top of an open hill and then just dry up. We are experienced walkers and we always have adequate provisions with us in case we get really lost, but although we have gone wrong often we always manage to get ourselves back on course. There is no point getting worked up or anxious. This is just another of those adventures that living in Bulgaria throws at you. Marieluise is always on the lookout for new places to ride and as we walk she is constantly assessing whether she could pass on horseback. Sometimes we must look quite dangerous because she insists we always carry a machete in case a track, that is otherwise suitable for horses, has become overgrown in parts. I am then called upon to hack my way through it while she investigates an easier route. It is exciting and hugely enjoyable.

As the summer gives way to autumn we spend more and more evenings at home. We have made the house very cosy, something for which Marieluise has a particular talent, and friends and family that have been here say they can see similarities to Silver Rake in the way the house is appointed. We are now well organised for evenings at home. We both love to read and although we prefer to hold a book in our hands we have taken to using Kindles as the local supply of English books would have been exhausted long ago. We like to watch good dramas on TV and the autumn season on British TV is particularly good. After trying every which way to watch British Television we now record programmes on our computer off a site called Filmon.com and watch them on a large monitor.

We have a good supply of local wine and Bulgarian beer so evenings are very pleasant. I recently e-mailed a friend at home, Dave, to say I had been paying forty pence a pint for my beer, of which he was already jealous, but I had now found a place where it could be bought for eighteen pence! A very good bottle of wine costs two pounds so evenings in are cheap as well as enjoyable. Sometimes Mandi and Keith join us and we particularly like sitting outside by the fire pit that we have built with a drink and some simple food putting the world, or at least Bulgaria, to rights. We all regard ourselves as very lucky.

Printed in Great Britain
by Amazon